SHAMELESS
15 Women Share Their Journey of
Self-Awareness, Self-Love, and
Leading with Light

CONTENT WARNING: Suicidal thoughts, sexual violence/discussion of rape, stalking or harassment, abuse, sex with a minor/harm to a child, eating disorders, miscarriage, emotional abuse, body shaming, female oppression, sex trafficking

SHAMELESS

15 Women Share Their Journey of
Self-Awareness, Self-Love, and
Leading with Light

An Imprint of Leschenault Press
Copyright © Leschenault Press, 2023
First Published: 2022 by Lisa Anderson Media, LLC
This edition published 2023 by Leschenault Press
Leschenault, Western Australia

ISBN: 978-1-923020-20-7 - Paperback Edition
ISBN: 978-1-923020-21-4 - Hardback Edition
ISBN: 978-1-923020-22-1- E-book Edition

All rights reserved.

The individual Author of each contribution to this anthology is the sole copyright owner of their particular Work, and retains all rights to the individual Work except for those expressly granted to Leschenault Press within and in association with this anthology.

This book deals with significant subject matter that may cause mental anguish, triggers, or other forms of trauma. If affected by the material within, it is recommended the reader seek help and assistance from a qualified medical, mental health, or other appropriate professional.

The Publisher and Authors jointly or singularly, accept no responsibility or liability for any damage, loss, or expense incurred as a result of the work contained within.

No part of this publication may be reproduced; stored in a retrieval system; copied in any form or by any means–electronic, mechanical, photocopying, recording or otherwise transmitted without written permission from the Publisher. You must not circulate this book in any format.

Dedication

To the leaders of light—the light bringers—thank you for your bravery. Your courage is seen. Your courage is admired. Your story is heard.

Profits/Royalties (or Author's Fees) are donated to
501(C)(3) NON-PROFITS

CONTENTS

Introduction 01
BY LISA ANDERSON, PUBLISHER

SECTION ONE 5

A Body Breaking into Self-Love 07
BY LAURA FLORES

The Girl with True Grit 15
BY JODI ANDERSON

Journey into the Soul 23
BY KHADÍJIH MITCHELL-POLKA

My All-America City and Me 31
BY DR. MANAL FAKHOURY

A Tale of Three Hospitals 39
BY SYDNEY RAFFERTY

The Bully Who Got Better 47
BY JACQUELINE KORPELA

SECTION TWO 55

Growing Through the Rearview Mirror 57
BY LAUREN DEBICK

Where the Real Power Is 65
BY KATERINA MACKENZIE

My Life is Mine to Write 73
BY ESMIRNA CARABALLO

Shattered but Not Broken 79
BY DANA (OLMSTEAD) KRULL

In Case of Emergency, Break Glass 85
BY SHEREESE FLOYD

From Victimhood to Warriorhood 93
BY CONNIE ROSE

Salvaged Soul 101
BY FANNIE OCASIO

Ride or Die 109
BY WENDY MESTAS

Send Me Courage in My Fear 115
BY JEANNE HENNINGSEN

INTRODUCTION

by Lisa Anderson, Publisher

I sat on the floor of the small, boxy room I shared with my older sister. The room was divided by bunkbeds, and I leaned on the bottom bunk as I stared intently at the cover of a Shania Twain CD. Flicking open the jewel case, I pulled out the booklet and began to thumb through the pages. Now and then, I would stop and stare at her picture. Maybe if I looked long enough and dreamed big enough, I would become her.

My fingers ran through my hair. Silky, sure, but straight as a stick. I stood in front of a full-length mirror, my body morphing into an ugly monster. No, I would never look like Shania.

☙ • ❧

The shame I felt about my body had grown like a cancer, and it was fed by bullies and witnessing the lack of self-confidence in other women in my family.

In high school, one of my closest friends was an athlete with beautiful olive skin, long curly hair, and legs for days. She was strong and beautiful, but it wasn't until our senior year she confided in me about her battle with bulimia.

I never confessed to her that I would regularly take handfuls of diet pills and painkillers.

Another friend suffered from a different body image complex. Naturally thin, she was often accused of being too skinny, and adults would shove cake and burgers at her, while they would tell me I shouldn't have a second helping.

My low self-esteem led to a series of bad relationships. One relationship had been plagued with emotional and sexual abuse. While I openly discussed the emotional trauma that had kept me tied to a man all my friends and family despised, I had refused to acknowledge the sexual abuse for almost twenty years.

❦

In 2008, after years of yo-yo diets and trying to recover from the abuse, my body developed a new symptom: extreme fatigue. It was devastating to my personality. I battled stomach pains and body aches, and I was constantly fighting to maintain or lose weight. I even became a strict vegan in 2019 in the hopes it would help me. It relieved some issues, but not for long, and other issues, like my fatigue, persisted. Doctors ignored or blamed me for my symptoms, and I still battle with many of the issues today.

However, in 2020, the pandemic swept the nation and changed the course of my life. Having been furloughed from a reputable media company, I started a magazine. It was during this journey I discovered a level of confidence I had never experienced, and I was reminded of the importance and power of stories.

Thinking back over my life, listening to the stories of other people, and feeling the need to pull together a community of women, I launched the idea for this book.

Eager to share as many stories as I could, I originally wanted forty women to tell their story. Surely, there were forty women who had been shamed, bullied, or emotionally or physically abused. Indeed, this is all too common, but it takes profound courage to discuss it and to be a light in the dark for the women who are still going through it. Not everyone is ready for that voyage, and that's okay.

The fifteen women who eagerly (and some tentatively) raised their hand are braver than you could imagine. Yet, everyone involved with this book agrees if it helps even one woman to step out of her current situation or realize she is not alone in her struggles, then the effort it took to be a part of this project was worth it.

Many of these stories will make you catch your breath. If you haven't been in a similar situation as the person in the story, you might even be quick to judge them for their decisions. It's easy to say you would do something different in their shoes, but I would ask you to take a step back and come to the table with an open mind.

I spent three years of my life experiencing trauma, and I still managed to victim-blame. Yes, I blamed myself, but I also judged other women in worse situations. "If he had ever physically abused me, I would have left," I would tell people. In the back of my mind, I knew he had both physically and emotionally abused me. My language eventually became "hit me," until one day, I realized I honestly didn't know if I would have left. Even if I had left, there was a good chance he would have talked me back into his life. Rinse and repeat—the pattern of physical and emotional abuse.

What amazes me more than the situations these women were put in or stayed in is the simple fact they are no longer in them. This includes the women who had challenges with mental health and body issues or were shamed or bullied. Pure grit, determination, and the willingness to lift other women up made it possible for them to sit down and share their stories with you.

᪥•᪣

Dear Reader,

    If you are in one of these situations right now, you are not alone and there is hope.

    Reach for the light-bringers, because they have forged a path in their darkest hours.

SECTION ONE

Breaking Free of Shame

1

A BODY BREAKING INTO SELF-LOVE

by Laura Flores

There are sounds that jolt you awake, like the sound of your alarm whirring in your bedroom on a day when you're deep in sleep. But the sound I heard on that night in 2018 was a different kind of sound. It's a sound I'll never forget. A bundle of sounds that came with the force of a freight train: a metallic crack, screeching rubber on concrete, the full-bodied blast of two cars colliding in the night, three lives changing in an instant. These are the sounds you never want to hear, but I can't say it didn't lead to the best possible outcome—one I couldn't have imagined.

After the accident, a lot of things changed for the better. But first, there was pain. The hill must be climbed before we can savor the view. So, there were growing pains. The pains of a woman stumbling into healing, a journey that would take every ounce of strength I had and every bit of courage and fortitude. Courage is not fun to muster. No one ever said courage was easy, and there's a reason for that. But sometimes, courage is the only way.

ಬ•ಲ

I was raised in a big family in Texas. My parents were short on money but full of expectations. I wanted to make them proud, to be a high achiever. I had a deep desire to please them. Sometimes, I took drastic measures. At thirteen, I began purging. Back then, there wasn't much talk about eating disorders. The famous singer Karen Carpenter suffered from anorexia, and although she and her eating disorder were in the spotlight, bulimia was not. It wasn't starvation. It wasn't cutting calories or making a meal of carrot sticks and diet colas. Bulimia was easier to hide. I could eat school lunches and family meals. Later, I could make it all go away with a trip to the bathroom. Poof, just like that, and no one was the wiser.

At sixteen, I was thin, and I enjoyed the fanfare. When my parents praised me, when anyone said, "Wow! you look good!" I held onto the words. I let the compliments feed me. They became my food. Friends were doing it anyway, so purging didn't feel like a problem. It was a solution. I had learned the art of maintaining beauty. The bent posture, the sharp poke of my finger like a needle jabbing a balloon. And then the rush of control, the release, the sensation of freeing my demon, being exorcised like the girl from the horror film. The youngest in my family, I was making my mark. I was the fit girl, not the fat girl.

I took my body for granted, but what I've learned is this: I can be fit and not healthy, not okay on the inside where it counts. But those are the parts no one can see. And when I'm slender with a lovely physique, no one wonders about my inner self. They assume I have everything under control, because I'm disciplined enough to keep my body in top shape. The truth is, I was addicted to the purge, the feeling of a hollow stomach. My empty center felt like an empty world—free of chaos—a world I could control and rule over. When people said, "You're beautiful," they had no idea I was killing myself slowly. They couldn't see the self-destruction. I tucked my hands into my pockets to hide the teeth marks on my knuckles.

My grandmother had become suspicious, and she began talking to my mother about my condition. Mom knew by then, too. Perhaps, she just didn't know what to do with a daughter who spent hours behind the bathroom door, hours working out with the homemade bench set my father had made me out of wood from the hardware store. I curled water bottles and pumped plastic until my palms were red and my whole body was slick with sweat. I was a dedicated athlete, determined to stay thin, no matter the cost. And while I thought I was headed toward a positive goal, I was an arrow flying in the wrong direction.

୭•ଓ

Dehydration, heart palpitations, low pulse, weakened muscles, and extreme fatigue. I had a beautiful body that I was breaking, but I couldn't stop myself. At night, I lay in bed counting the calories I'd consumed and wondering if I'd purged enough. I thought about the dizzy spells, the blackouts, and the physical signs that terrified me but weren't enough to make me change my ways. I was more afraid of weight gain than of passing out or putting stress on my heart. When I looked in the mirror, I saw the broken blood vessels under my eyes like tiny spokes on a bicycle wheel. I saw the sharp contours of my body, my bones jutting out here and there. But I was proud of what I had made. Like a sculptor with a hunk of clay, my body was my creation. As much as I thought I loved myself, though, my behavior was an act of self-loathing.

I understood all about loving others, about the Golden Rule and what it meant to be a good girl, because the world doesn't need more trouble. No one ever said, "Love yourself." No one ever said, "You can't possibly be a light, if you're living in darkness." I kept my fears bottled up inside, my insecurities churning in my gut. But when I purged, I felt it all fall away for a moment. I was free.

My grandmother continued to warn my mother about my obsessive behavior. One day, Mom drove me to see a doctor in Rio Grande Valley. The drive was a blur of traffic and stoplights, billboards, and the buzzing city. I listened to the hum of the motor, watched Mom's hands gripping the wheel. We were silent as the radio played early Nineties hits. When we pulled into the parking lot, I saw patients hobbling into the building—seniors with fuzzy gray hair, nursing their walkers and canes. Mom had taken me to see a geriatric doctor. What would this man know about a bulimic teen?

They poked me with needles and filled tiny vials with my bright red blood. They put me on the scale and slid the metal bar until it teetered below the one hundred mark. The nurse scribbled a number in the manila file she was holding. When the doctor entered the room, he asked my mother a series of questions, as if I couldn't speak for myself. I resented him and the entire visit. I didn't want to think about my blood, my heart, or any of my other organs. I was young and invincible, too young to be sitting in a geriatric doctor's office.

The doctor pressed a cold stethoscope to my heart and listened to the faded thump, shaking his head and narrowing his eyes behind a cheap pair of wire-rimmed glasses. He proceeded with his tests and headshakes and then finally said to my mother, "Do you realize how low her potassium levels are? She could have a heart attack."

Mom folded her hands in her lap, snapped her head around, and gave me a hard look.

There were more doctors after that first visit, and then, there was counseling. But I never really dug deep and addressed the issues that were fueling my addiction. I refused to change the lifestyle that allowed me to mold my body into what I thought was beautiful.

I was bulimic in my homecoming dress. I was bulimic throughout four pregnancies. I was bulimic when I had a miscarriage. Bulimia played a major role in my life for the next three decades. I attempted to heal myself through routines. I had a happy marriage, but my lack of self-love and self-esteem ran too deep to change. By the time I was forty-six, I'd spent most of my life wrestling with my eating disorder. I forgot that life is fragile; I was about to learn a hard lesson.

ಬ•ಲ

The accident broke me in every sense of the word. The jolt was incredible.

My car had thirty-two airbags, and all of them deployed. I remember the sounds and the way time stretched out, as if the car careening toward us was actually crawling and not doing 80 mph. It was 2018, and I was leaving my parents' house with my twelve-year-old son. My husband had just called about meeting for dinner.

I was exhausted and in my workout clothes, so I wanted to eat at home. It was almost 9:00 p.m., and the roads were dark. I turned right to leave my parents' gated neighborhood, and there he was—seemingly out of nowhere—the drunk man in the Pontiac. I flung my arm in front of my son, the way moms do.

The man had run a red light. I had a second to choose whether to brace myself, brake, or gun it. I can't say if it was just my own mind working overtime, but I heard my father's voice: "Go with it." Dad was still alive, but somehow, he was my angel that night. Looking back, I understand how those other options could have proved fatal. Braking would have exposed the passenger's side of the car and my son. Hitting the gas would have put the impact on my gas tank—potentially causing an explosion. There was no room for error.

I don't recall going to the hospital, I only remember the sheets, the stiff mattress, the overhead lights, and the gaping windows. Someone in a set of scrubs said, "blunt force trauma and internal injuries," but all I heard was that my body was broken and I wouldn't be allowed at the gym. Fitness was the other side of my addiction. The gym was my safe place. It was empowering, like purging. It was how I had coped with life every day, and now, it was ripped away. What would I do, but more importantly, who would I be without the tools I'd used to control my body, my world?

I was angry at the driver who got behind the wheel that night. Angry at the doctors, my body, the new road ahead. I had resigned myself to the fact that bulimia was okay, exercise addiction was okay. My life was okay. I closed my eyes, clenched my fists and felt the heat of my anger erupt in my chest. There'd be no more distractions now. I had nothing but time to reflect.

The weight piled on like I knew it would. With internal injuries and a broken body, I could no longer purge. I couldn't lift weights or run marathons. Some days, I could barely lift my head. But when I thought about what might have happened, how my son and I could have been killed, a sense of gratitude snuffed out the angry fire in my chest. "That's it," I whispered to my body. Gratitude would get me through this.

They came in waves—gratitude and joy—but there were other emotions, too, and I had to wade in all of it as I moved toward healing. I felt helpless and lost at times. Sharp pains came and went, and I needed sleep, food, and courage to stay the course. After several months, I was strong enough to rush to the bathroom, to throw my body into that old familiar position, fingers poking at my throat. But I didn't. It took all the energy I could muster to stay put, to sit with the food in my belly and the overwhelming urge to purge. Sometimes, my hand shook like an alcoholic at a bar, contemplating the options. But each time I didn't purge, it got easier. Soon, bulimia was a speck in my rearview, so small I could barely see it.

When the doctors said it's okay to return to the gym, I gnawed on the tips of my fingers. Those were the words I'd been waiting to hear, but now I was afraid of what I might do. Could I handle a workout without turning fitness into an obsession, an addiction? I had to set boundaries, to find a way to self-regulate. But how?

☙ • ❧

Some people slip into your life for a reason. They help you become who you're supposed to be.

I was single, in my twenties, and running a tanning salon when I met Jack. We were instant friends. He was confident, well-groomed, a silk tie-and-pressed suit kind of guy. He said looking good wasn't about making an impression. It was about self-care, self-love, and treating your body with respect. That was such a foreign concept for me—looking good because you felt good and wanted your appearance to match your mindset. Jack helped me see myself as an individual, not as just a woman.

He told me I had potential. The same was true about him. He had depth, a fighting spirit. He'd say, "I know I look self-absorbed, but I care about me." When no one else would see the circles under my eyes or my bruised knuckles from vomiting, Jack would, and he'd remind me of the importance of my life—of my children. He'd make me laugh during a time when tears usually filled my eyes. Little did I know that inside, he was struggling, too. He was the last person I'd expected to take his own life. But in 2014, he did.

His suicide shocked me to the core, but I had buried the memory of him, buried my grief. In the aftermath of my accident, though, Jack's words began to haunt me, despite the fact he'd been gone for years. When I had time to reflect and think, his voice gained volume and strength. The dormant conversations we shared flooded back in an instant. They gave me courage when everything ached.

When I looked in the mirror, I saw a worn-out woman. I was out of shape and emotionally drained. I was bruised—a physical therapy patient, who spent my days shuffling in and out of doctor's offices, and praying to be healthy and whole, while fighting the urge to grow bitter and give up the fight. I had to be a mom, a daughter, and a wife. How could I focus on my own transformation?

Still hearing the faint voice of my friend in my ear, I decided to take a bold, scary step: enroll in life coaching courses.

The curriculum was daunting, more rigorous than I ever imagined with education on everything from phytonutrients to facilitating client insight and offering tools and techniques for a powerful mindset. I pored over textbooks at the library, reading so hard and so long my eyes blurred the words into blobs of ink. And while I tried to keep his voice in the forefront, my own self-doubt began to creep in.

One particularly grueling day, I spent hours at the library opening my books, slamming them shut, opening them again, as I gripped my pen. I looked around at the rows of books, worn-out spines, and faded covers. In that cavernous place, I listened to the sound of pages turning, of stacks of books clunking down on the counter, the librarian scanning their codes. I had a homesick feeling, like a child on the first day of school. What was I doing here, and why did I think I could pull this off? And life and health coaching? Who was I to be anyone's coach? My thoughts made loops in my mind. I wriggled in my seat, took deep breaths, and tried to focus.

I walked over to the coffee shop beside the library, hoping to distract my buzzing brain. The wide windows soaked up the afternoon sun. I walked around, watching the people around me: a woman rifling through her handbag. A man fixed on his phone, clutching a paper cup. I felt my courage waning. I should pack up and go, I thought. This was a mistake. Just then, a gentleman walked by, and I caught a whiff of his cologne. It was like a cold slap of water, an awakening. He was wearing Jack's cologne. Immediately, the scent brought me back to him. I felt his presence, heard his voice saying, "You got this."

He'd known me as a shy girl, an introvert. He was a public speaker, but he knew how I felt. He said, "Laura, every time I grab the microphone, I'm in shock and in fear. But I do it afraid. I do it to motivate myself." Motivation isn't a feeling. It's a decision. Right then, I made up my mind. I would believe in my own potential. I went back to my table and opened my book. I needed this course to motivate me, to give me strength and knowledge, so I could change other people's lives like Jack changed mine.

ಏ•ಐ

"Bulimia was a problem, but it wasn't the root of the problem," I told the reporter. She was interviewing me for a local story. Talking to her was good practice for my next speaking gig. I was sponsoring The Miss & Mrs. World Texas 2021 event and was named the year's official health coach.

"A lack of self-love was where the core issues were," I continued. "Once I had dealt with that, I was able to break free from my addictions."

The process of becoming a life and health coach finally allowed me to truly see myself. My inner child emerged from a cocoon and into a beautiful, healthy inside and out, dedicated woman. Through helping others, I learned I was enough. I also saw that I was not alone in my struggles. Finally, I had found hope in my life. This was me—reformed, reinvented, renewed. Jack wanted me to love myself. At forty-nine years old, I finally do. I'm ready to live.

ABOUT THE AUTHOR

LAURA FLORES

Laura Flores is a certified transformational life and health coach, helping clients break bad habits. When she's not working out at the gym or motivating others, she enjoys the feel of her hands in the dirt as she tends to her butterfly garden. She believes there's no greater joy than achieving your goals and reaching your highest potential. After years of struggling with bulimia, she is proud to be a shameless woman who tells her story to inspire others to find courage and hope on their journey. Visit www.justdoitlifecoaching.com to learn more.

2

THE GIRL WITH TRUE GRIT

by Jodi Anderson

I clutched the paper Groupon voucher nervously, as I walked into CrossFit Zoo. I had a vague idea that CrossFit was some kind of workout, and this warehouse was actually a gym (or "box," in CrossFit parlance). It smelled of chalk, sweat, and hot rubber mats. The industrial fans kept air circulating in the otherwise un-air-conditioned space. It was June in Florida. It was hot.

The first workout with owner and coach Shae was box jumps and ball slams. She set down the smallest platform, like the one used in aerobics videos, and handed me an eight-pound rubber ball. The hard rock music kicked in, and when she counted 3-2-1, I jumped. After my last jump, I stepped off the platform and onto the pint-sized medicine ball and fell over. I flailed like a flipped tortoise, my thigh muscles too wobbly to support me. Shae, two inches shorter than me, hauled me up from the floor. I was 34, obese, and horribly out of shape.

CrossFit calls their members "athletes." I had never been mistaken for an athlete. The next day, despite being unable to stand up from the toilet without hanging on to the sink just the night before, I walked back into the box. I saw a middle-aged guy doing handstand push-ups, and I almost turned around. I was sure I was in the wrong place. Who was I kidding?

Children form beliefs about themselves at a very early age, and those beliefs go on to inform their willingness to try new things or stick to a difficult task. From then on, they see only that they have failed at the task they believed they could not do. And they become adults who believe themselves failures. Every subsequent failure further confirms their belief, a phenomenon called "confirmation bias."

In elementary school, I was tormented by my peers and a sadistic gym teacher. I was picked dead last for kickball and was the first target of any dodgeball-type game. If I'd ever had a shred of belief in my potential athleticism, it died on the day we did tumbling in fifth-grade gym class.

I was determined to learn how to do a back bend from a standing position, so two days before the event, I practiced with my one friend Sarah—over and over and over. I was so proud when I could finally do it! But when the day came to perform my gymnastics routine, I had forgotten to memorize it. I was terribly stiff from all the practicing, and I had worn the worst clothes possible: baggy jeans and a soft, white sweater with a large collar (not really in fashion, even in the Eighties) that flew in my face every time I bent over.

Another classmate was instructed to read my routine to me. Cartwheel. Forward somersault. Round-off. With every skill, I had to pull up my pants and push the sweater away from my face. My throat tightened, and my eyes welled up, tears threatening to spill over. I was a crier, but I did not want to give my audience the satisfaction. Backwards somersault. I started sweating, which caused my collar to stick to my neck. Finally, the back bend. But I could not do it from the standing position. I lay down on the blue mat. I could smell the plastic and myself. I pushed up into a back bend and let myself down again. I got up awkwardly, trying to ignore the giggles coming from the stage. I rose, flushed with embarrassment, and found a seat on the steps.

But my humiliation was not over when I finished my routine. Mr. Neste recorded the whole class and gave the VHS tape to the regular classroom teacher, who showed it in a free period. My classmates had a second laugh at my expense. I was not an athlete. I would never be an athlete.

A lack of athleticism was not the only belief I had about myself. I knew I was smart, but other kids were smart. I was also weird. I cried when I got questions wrong on schoolwork. I preferred the company of adults. I did not connect well with other kids my age. I believed I was fat my entire childhood. Because I was rejected by most of the kids in my class, I took the belief that I was an "acquired taste" into my adulthood, convinced that people who liked me were either deluded or weird, too.

Shae talked me into staying at her gym, into investing in myself with my meager income from the part-time job I worked while earning my education degree. Two weeks later, I did eighty squats hanging on to a pole for support, with everyone who had finished the workout before me cheering me on.

"Come on, Jodi! You can do this!"

"You've got this, Jodi! Keep going!"

No one laughed. I was last, but when I finished, I collected fist bumps and high-fives.

Bit by bit, my strength increased, along with my confidence, until one day, I pushed a one-hundred-pound barbell over my head. I was ecstatic! I liked feeling strong. If I could become an athlete, what else could I do? I carried myself differently. I started to believe I could succeed at hard things.

My life was full of hard things, or at least, things that seemed harder for me than for others. At sixteen, I started to experience depression. I thought it was because the guy I liked rejected me. And whenever I felt depressed, I believed it was a lack of faith in God's plan for me. When my beloved, uncle died of complications related to alcohol abuse, my college GPA plummeted, and I dropped out after two semesters. I made rash decisions, like moving across the country without a job or a place to live—all my belongings packed into a blue 1986 Mazda 626. I could not hold on to a job for long. I moved again. And again. At twenty-one, I contemplated suicide.

Eventually, my depression eased. I did not follow through on my suicidal ideation, and I credited my involvement in my church. In 2003, I went back to school. I chose Calvin College, a Christian school in Michigan. But I kept struggling with depression. Why could I not have faith that it would work out? I feared I was disappointing God. I went to see a counselor on campus. She suggested that maybe I needed some medication.

I was so relieved. I was going to get better! I was not a failure. There was something wrong with me, but it was not my fault. It was not a character flaw.

A family doctor diagnosed me with moderate depression and put me on an anti-depressant. I began falling asleep in classes. When I was awake, I could not think straight. My head buzzed. I walked out on a test in my favorite class—something I never, in my wildest dreams, thought I would have done. I just could not remember anything we'd read. My professors were understanding, but between my tenuous financial situation and my mental health struggles, I dropped out at the end of the year.

My diagnosis was wrong, and the wrong medication only made me worse. Two years later, I would be properly diagnosed by a psychiatrist in Madison, Wisconsin, where I had moved in with my best girl friend from my first college. I finally got a good job working for the university and had health insurance. I did not have moderate depression; I had bipolar II disorder.

Bipolar II disorder is characterized by periods of depression with short periods of mania, called hypomania. Most people experience the mania as euphoria. My personal joke is that I don't get even the good parts of my disorder: I have dysphoric episodes. I get irritable, irrational. I cannot concentrate. In Grand Rapids, I had started to self-medicate when my episodes would come on. If I were drunk, my brain slowed down. (This was not a winning strategy.) The anti-depressants treated my depression and made the mania worse. The psychiatrist put me on a combination of a mood stabilizer and an anti-psychotic. We had to adjust the dosages a bit, but he hit the bull's eye. I started getting better.

On medication, my bipolar is manageable. I am less depressed and even have a lot of good days. My manic episodes are now restricted to once or twice a year. They last for about four days. On day one, I begin to get irritable. I snipe without provocation. On the second day, my brain starts to whirl. I feel like I'm sitting in the Gravitron, that carnival ride that goes round and round. I have never ridden one, but I imagine it's like that: pressed against the wall by the force of gravity, waiting for the spinning to end. I can't work. I can't do much of anything, except lie down and watch TV, until it's over in a day or two. Then, the fatigue comes, as if the mania sapped all my energy, leaving me as motivated as a wet wash cloth.

My healing began with compassion towards myself. That poor girl. She did not know why she was depressed. She did not know why she did weird things, like go out to rent a video and then drive to the next town, get lost, then drive back and go to the local movie theater to see *Cold Mountain*, when her roommates were expecting her back in a few minutes, rather than several hours. (Jen punched me in the boob and ordered me never to do that again.) And now I knew why: I had a mental illness.

Everything was great from then on, right? The medication, the counseling, a city I loved. I got married to my best guy friend. We moved to Florida to escape the brutal winters and be closer to my dad, who offered my husband a full-time job at his growing online retail business. I enrolled in an online secondary education program to (finally) earn my bachelor's degree.

But I wasn't a new person. As things fell apart much the same as they had before—this time, a failed marriage in addition to getting fired from terrible jobs—I continued to struggle with depression and the sense that I just could not change. I could not get better. I might not be suffering quite so much from deep depression and my mania was not ambushing me several times a week, but I was still suffering.

I was used to suffering, though. If I have a super power, it is grit. Sometimes, that can be bad: I tend to hang on to jobs in which I am miserable, until I get fired for poor performance. I stayed in a bad marriage for too long. But more often than not, my ability to "suffer," to hang in there, is good—like graduating summa cum laude while going through a divorce or taking my first teaching gig at a Level 6 correctional facility for male juveniles. Those were really hard things! Moving from a liberal, over-educated city to a smaller, conservative, low-education suburb-to-nowhere was a difficult transition, but I have made a home here. To this day, I remain best friends with my ex-husband. I can do hard things. I have grit.

There are days, though, when I lament the need to have grit. Why do I have to grit my teeth to push through when others can simply walk ahead? What is wrong with me? For most of my life, that question has resounded in my head and heart: What is wrong with me? What is my moral failing? I no longer believe that I am disappointing God, but I still hold on to the guilt and shame of failure. I am in my forties with no career, making just enough to get by with a roommate to help pay the bills. Surely, I am as smart as my more successful friends! What went wrong?

The answer to this question shocked me. And it came about as a result of preparing to write this chapter. I have a journey out of shame. I have worked very hard to accept myself—mental illness and all—and have learned the art of forgiveness and grace...mostly. And I love to share that journey with others who struggle with self-acceptance and -love. And that's what I intended to write about. I did not intend to have a life changing revelation—that I have attention deficit hyperactive disorder (ADHD).

When I overlay my diagnosis onto my life, it makes so much sense. How did I get to middle age before getting diagnosed? ADHD is missed in 50 to 75 percent of girls. That's right: Up to three in four of us are walking around with stuff we blame on our flawed character. (There are those ingrained beliefs, again.) People commonly envision hyperactivity as the main symptom of ADHD—like that boy who could *never* sit still—but girls, like me, more often have inattentive type. We are the daydreamers, the breakers of dishware, the "bad" drivers, the interrupters of conversation, the disorganized scatterbrains.

To top it off, depression and anxiety co-occur with ADHD in up to 30 percent of us. Those symptoms can mask the symptoms of ADHD, causing them to be overlooked entirely. That's why my bipolar II disorder was caught, but my other disorder was missed.

How did ADHD present itself in my childhood? I was what my mother called a "sensitive child." I cried a lot, especially when I failed at something or perceived failure. That is what is now known as emotional disregulation; when I got overwhelmed, I had very big feelings, like when I embarrassed myself with my tumbling routine. This tendency made me a social pariah, and I had few friends, none by the sixth grade. I had a difficult time connecting with my peers and preferred conversations with adults. I carried a book around and lost myself in those fictional worlds to the exclusion of all else. People would have to tap me to get my attention, because I did not hear them. I was hyperfocused, another ADHD trait.

My intelligence was my favorite attribute; I was singled out as "gifted." Because I was such a good student, teachers missed the signs of my disorder. I had an extensive vocabulary at an early age. (My mother tells the story that, when I was four, she was getting my sister and me ready to go grocery shopping, and I suddenly announced, "We are going to go forth and explore!") I didn't read early, but by the first grade, I was reading at a fifth-grade level. I earned straight As for almost my entire school career, and in the sixth grade, I tested post-high school on standardized tests. In high school, I was inducted into the National Honors Society.

If I had been properly diagnosed, I would have been labeled "twice exceptional," a gifted student with a mental disorder (or two). But that term did not get coined until the Nineties, when I was a teenager. I got pulled out of my regular elementary school classroom to work with someone because I was special, but I did not get assistance for my disability. What I took away from that experience was that, although I was smart, I could not get my life together to reach my potential.

Getting into CrossFit taught me I could be something I never thought I could be. If I could change that one thing about myself, I could change others. And if I were an athlete, now, maybe I had always been an athlete. What other beliefs were wrong?

I started looking at my past through a lens of understanding. I had a mental illness that made my life difficult. I began to forgive myself for failing to meet my own high, maybe unattainable, standards. When things got difficult, when I became ill or injured and had to recover my fitness, I reminded myself that if I had done it once, I could do it again. When I fell into depression, I reminded myself that I could get out again. I had grit.

The ADHD diagnosis is the final piece. I had so many struggles that I could not attribute to the bipolar disorder. After getting properly medicated, I should have gotten better at being a productive adult, I thought. And when I didn't, I wondered if maybe I did have a character flaw I just could not perfect. Now, I have the whole picture; I have solved the puzzle.

It feels like I have forgiven myself, and yet, there was nothing to forgive. With understanding comes relief and acceptance. A big weight has fallen from my shoulders. The weight was my expectations and the guilt and shame from the failure to meet those expectations.

I still have so much work to do. I have to begin to break down and reconstruct my beliefs about my past and the stories I told myself about who I am. I have to unlearn unhealthy coping mechanisms that I put in place to protect myself. I must peel away the mask I've worn to make myself socially acceptable and meet my true self. It will not be easy. But if there is one thing I know about myself, it is this: I can do hard things.

ABOUT THE AUTHOR

JODI ANDERSON

Jodi Anderson is Senior Copy Editor for Lisa Anderson Media and an aspiring author. She strives to live authentically, promote body positivity, and normalize talking about mental health. She is an unabashed cat lady and mama to Dickens, Freya, and Tux. They all currently reside in Ocala, Florida.

3

JOURNEY INTO THE SOUL

by Khadíjih Mitchell-Polka

Growing up, I always had a sense that there was more than meets the eye when it came to existence. From a young age, I was sensitive to emotion and vibration and was certain I could see spirits from beyond the veil. However, because of my own conditioning, I began to suppress and block my spiritual gifts at some point. Even still, the inner knowing that there must be something beyond what I could observe in my physical reality carried me through many moments when I wanted to give up. This soft whisper in my heart helped me find strength to repeatedly get up, dust myself off, and keep going.

I grew up in a world of lack, where there was never enough time, money, or love, but there was always more than enough stress, pain, and hardship. My mother was a kindergarten teacher and sole financial provider for our family of eight. My father was a stay-at-home dad and aspiring writer, who never quite fulfilled his dream. From the role my mother played, I witnessed and learned patience, courage, dedication, and passion. From my father, I learned acceptance, understanding, and forgiveness. My parents raised me and my siblings as Bahá'í, and from a young age there was a large element of living a life of faith at home. To me, my parents' devotion to the Bahá'í Faith was the silver lining that held our family together.

Despite our spiritual ties, life at home was often chaotic and unpredictable. My father, who suffered from depression, bipolar disorder, and various health issues, was knee-deep in a battle with his shadow. On some days, he was more cognizant of it than on others. There were numerous times when what he was fighting in his inner world became a projection onto his assumptions about who my siblings and I were. Many days, it seemed as though we were walking on eggshells and never really knew what to expect.

To escape the turmoil I felt at home, I would hang out with my friends as often as I could. I had a few close friends that I stuck to like glue and found comfort in their companionship, as they mirrored my awkward and goofy nature. At school, though, I often felt out of place with many of the other kids. There were multiple times in elementary school when I was teased for my strange name and shamed for the second-hand clothes I wore and being vegetarian, white trailer park trash, and a Bahá'í.

My grandpa and mom enrolled me in ballet at the age of eight. At first, this was truly a bright spot, but ballet eventually spotlighted the trauma I was holding in my body. It was the summer after sixth grade, and I had been dancing for roughly four years. Over the summer, we'd gone on a family vacation, and I had put on some weight. It was my first day back to dance after vacation, and I had gotten dressed in my usual attire of leotard and tights. I was walking out of my parents' bathroom, when my dad called me over and said, "Khadíjih, don't you think you are getting a little pudgy around the middle?" I couldn't tell you what happened after that, but that moment became imprinted on my mind and aided in cultivating a new identity for me.

I am certain if my father had known the effect those words would have on me, he never would have said them. While his words did not affect me immediately, they seeped into my subconscious and went to work. Over the next year, I became more involved in ballet and my dream of one day becoming a professional ballerina. With my father's words and images of thin ballerinas lingering in the backdrop of my mind, it was not long before I concluded that food was the enemy, and my weight was going to hold me back from my dreams.

Slowly, I stopped eating and spent the next four years dancing my heart out and hiding my secret friend, anorexia. Dance became my escape, and what I ate felt like the only thing I could control. Any time my weight went over 100 pounds, I would feel ashamed and remind myself how unworthy I was of being a ballerina. I would spend hours in front of the mirror, putting myself down for how ugly I was, prodding different areas of my body, and crying about how I wished I could be perfect.

When I was sixteen, during the first week of a Summer Intensive with the Colorado School of Ballet, weighing eighty-seven pounds at five feet, seven inches tall, I finally came clean to my parents. Along with this outing of my secret came an intense desire to get as far away from dance and anything else that resembled this part of my life. So, I left the intensive, traveled home, and ultimately quit dance altogether.

After that, everything changed. I didn't know who I was without dance. My family, friends, and doctors all told me I needed to "get better," but I had no clue what that meant. My time in ballet, my turbulent home life, and the prejudices passed on me for my faith, name, status, etc. conditioned me to believe I would never be enough, that I had to be perfect but never would be, that I was always doing something wrong, and that those who love me would likely hurt me. I felt confused, out of control, and alone, and all I wanted was to escape the life I was living.

☙•☜

Shortly after leaving dance, I moved out of my parents' house and began what I would later call "my darkest year." I dropped out of high school and did all I could to run from myself and the intense pain in the pit of my gut. I mingled with crowds that were not healthy for me, did drugs, and drank too much.

Then, the day after my eighteenth birthday, I found out I was pregnant. This was a defining moment in my life. I knew something had to change, if I were going to be a mother. I stopped drinking and doing hard drugs and found myself facing the fact that I would need to gain weight to carry a child.

I spent a lot of time with my dad when I was pregnant with my daughter. Even though he was physically ill and his body deteriorating, he made a point to call me at least once a week and would frequently pick me, so we could hang out. I knew he was worried about me and wanted to make sure I was okay. I was worried about me, too, and was grateful for the comfort his companionship provided. There were numerous times he said to me, "Don't worry about the weight you gain sweetie; you are caring for two, now." Perhaps, it was because I felt I had his approval, or maybe, because I was responsible for the growth of a child, but that was the first time in years I didn't agonize over the way my body looked as I put on weight.

It was during this time that I witnessed the true changes my father made as a person. From a young age, I had watched him work through his own traumas and conditioning with what seemed to be little progress. The difference between who he was at the end of his life and who he was when I was younger was night and day. Words cannot describe how grateful I am for this extended time I had with him. He passed away just three months after my daughter was born, and I have cherished these memories of him ever since. To this day, I am grateful he was my dad and for all he taught me. In truth, I feel more connected to him now that he is beyond the veil, and I know he continues to guide me as I walk through this lifetime.

About a year after my father's passing, I found myself pregnant with a second child, my son. Not long after that, I finally summoned the courage to leave the abusive relationship with my children's biological father. Out of respect for my children, I am choosing to leave the details of this out of the story, even though they have greatly impacted my journey to who I am today.

As I walked down the path of motherhood, I experienced moments of grief accompanied by overwhelming anger that reminded me all too much of my father when I was younger. Before becoming a mother, I resented, blamed, and felt abandoned by my father and wanted to hold him accountable for all my problems. Those feelings faded away after he passed, and I was a struggling, single, twenty-year-old mother of two. It was then that I recognized him in me and realized he had been doing the best he could with the tools he had been given. Even though I felt forgiveness for my father, I was just beginning the journey of releasing the trauma that had become stored in my body.

I put all my energy into making a life for me and my kids in the years that followed, but the stressors of being a single mother, fighting a custody battle, and living with buried trauma left me operating under intense anxiety and stress. Even still, I made the vow to always be a better mother today than I was yesterday and promised myself to keep working toward my healing. I have said many times that my children saved my life, because even when I didn't want to heal for myself, I always wanted to heal for them.

༄•༄

At the age of twenty-three, after three years in therapy, receiving my GED, and earning an associate degree in psychology, I found my way to physics and fell deeper into my spirituality. I spent the next 4.5 years working on my degree and following cookie crumbs from the Universe as to where I was headed. I didn't know why I was studying physics, but I felt a strong knowing that the Universe was guiding me. All I had to do was tune in and follow the dimly lit path ahead of me.

I found an amazing group of friends and met my soul sister, a woman who forever changed my world by accepting me as I was and mirroring my spiritual nature. I also began cycling and became involved with the local cycling community. For the first time, I felt at home in a town that, for so long, had felt like a prison.

Near the end of my program, I met my husband and after graduation we headed off into the "real world." By this time, my eating disorder felt like a thing of the past. I still struggled with my body image but no longer starved myself to lose weight. We moved away from home, and I began teaching high school mathematics and working on a master's in education. I used to call this first year away from home the "longest year" of my life. Not only had I left my friends and community behind, but I was ad hoc learning how to be a teacher and facing traumatic memories that were surfacing inside of me. I was once again overwhelmed by life and my past, but I had found a new resolve and dedication to healing.

I believe that this opportunity for healing came because I was in a stable relationship with a man who loved me without judgment. This allowed me to be vulnerable and to let go of my need for perfection. It was at this time that I also found Gabrielle Bernstein's *The Universe Has Your Back* and Eckhart Tolle's *The Power of Now*. These books brought me back to the power of the present moment and to that of surrendering to love. The wisdom shared helped me begin embracing my gifts of intuition and sight beyond the veil that I had once suppressed. More than ever before, I could feel my father's presence all around me, and I knew he was helping to guide me along a path I could not see.

Two years later, in 2018, my family and I headed north so I could begin a Ph.D. in education doing physics education research. From the start of the program, I found myself once again dancing with anxiety and high stress. Old, buried wounds of not belonging or being accepted stirred and became amplified once more. I nursed the belief that I was not enough and that something was wrong with me.

For the first eight months of the program, I felt under attack and was constantly operating in fight-or-flight mode. I didn't realize it, but I had stopped facing my trauma and was once again letting the past define me. Evidence of this appeared in the form of a chronic back injury that was diagnosed as minor scoliosis, degenerative disc disease, and herniated discs. Thus, my free time became preoccupied with a series of visits to physical therapists, massage/cupping therapists, primary care doctors, a chiropractor, a spine specialist, and a urologist, all in hopes that they could heal me.

By December 2019, experiencing little relief, I had stopped seeing most of my doctors and specialists. I found myself moving through a dark night of the soul, with a surfacing understanding that to heal my body, I had to release the trauma stored within it.

Upon the New Year, I summoned the courage to begin counseling using EMDR (Eye Movement Desensitization and Reprocessing) therapy. The time I spent in session was fruitful and helped me begin diving into myself to find true healing. Unfortunately, the therapy sessions were short-lived. The virus that touched the entire world made its way to our town, and the campus counseling center was physically closed.

After about two weeks of severe depression and no desire to do telehealth talk therapy, I was praying for a solution. So, when the Universe gifted me with a twenty-one-day meditation challenge from Deepak Chopra, I jumped at the opportunity.

My old ways of coping were no longer working, and I knew something had to change. I began the meditation challenge with an open heart for what it might bring. Within just two days, I felt a new sense of calm. After the first week, I was having moments of real happiness. After two weeks, I felt the depressing fog in my mind begin to lift. And at the three-week mark, I started to feel the sense of wholeness I had been longing for. I could feel the vibrant version of me rising from beneath the trauma, and I knew meditation was an important piece of my path forward.

My morning practice was working wonders on my well-being, and with each day, I could feel my focus shifting as I began refocusing my attention on love instead of fear. I was once again reminded of the deep knowing I had carried with me through the years: There is more beyond what I could observe in my physical reality.

The spring semester ended, and I met summer with anticipation and eagerness. I set the intention to dedicate the entire summer to my personal growth and healing. I spent hours in meditation, reading, writing, and willingly shedding old parts of me and the trauma in my body. With each day, I began feeling more like a different person, and the distraught, torn apart woman I had been felt further and further away.

As I asked for aid, the Universe reintroduced me to spiritual teachers, who had helped me through the years prior, along with new ones. As I prayed to be shown my next steps, I was blessed to find my Soul Tribe within the Global Coherence Pulse and Islands of Coherence. I began wholeheartedly embracing my spiritual gifts and honoring the qualities of myself I had once been ashamed of and shamed for.

I found myself no longer resonating with the desire to obtain a Ph.D. but, instead, felt called to walk in a new direction. I knew I was being called to be a teacher; however, I began realizing that I was not meant to teach in the traditional sense. My time studying physics and education had been connecting me with a deeper understanding of life and the Universe and preparing me for the independent journey I was to guide others on. I started my own business, Journey into the Soul LLC, and began work as a Meditation Guide & Intuitive Coach.

For a while, my ego tried to convince me to complete my Ph.D. while walking this new path. I felt torn, so I prayed for clarity and guidance. After months of deliberation, I was able to clearly hear the guidance of Spirit. I finally understood that the time had come to take the turn on my path, leave the Ph.D. behind, and embrace the unknown. So, I received a second masters, spent one final semester teaching my physics class, and set my focus on cultivating a vision I could feel but not see.

The Journey into my Soul has been the most important journey I could have ever embarked upon. The opportunity to truly heal has only been possible because I have been willing to take the less-traveled road within. The deeper I go, the more I excavate, and the clearer the path in front of me becomes. The more I honor the true knowing emanating from within my soul, the more I hear the call that I am here to guide others to do the same. With full faith and trust in the path I am on, I am dedicated to using my life experience, the guidance of Spirit, and the tools that have helped me heal to guide others on a journey into their soul.

ABOUT THE AUTHOR

KHADÍJIH MITCHELL-POLKA

A Meditation Guide & Intuitive Mentor, Khadíjih Mitchell-Polka has been a teacher and student for many years, formally studying in the areas of psychology, physics, mathematics, education, and yoga, and informally in mysticism, religion, spirituality, and various not yet widely accepted laws of the Universe, including consciousness, coherence, and the Law of Attraction. Khadíjih guides individuals to reconnect with their mind, body, and spirit. Learn more at www.journeyintothesoul.com and linktr.ee/journeyintothesoul

4

MY ALL-AMERICA CITY AND ME

by Dr. Manal Fakhoury

When I talk about what happened to me in the 2021 Ocala, Florida mayor's race, especially because I am Palestinian, especially because I am Muslim (and female), my voice still shakes with disbelief and disappointment. I know it's not a unique story for a Muslim woman to run up against prejudice and bigotry, but until the past several years, I had not experienced it myself. And it was vicious!

As hard and painful as it was for me, it also hurt many others, including my family, friends, and community.

When my family first moved to the US in the late 1960s, we found grace, not hate. In fact, when we moved from Los Angeles out to Moorpark in Ventura County, we were Moorpark's first Middle Eastern family, and we were hailed as pioneers.

Our introduction to English was our father teaching us to recite the Pledge of Allegiance by listening to a tape recorded by a neighbor. With that as our base, off we all went to school. For me, it was elementary school, where teachers were generous with their help and guidance, not only in the classroom, but also outside of the classroom. That was when I first felt the joy of joining, of belonging to a group with shared interests: the Brownies. The day my father took me to the store to buy my uniform was a high point.

My parents flourished as active members of the community, giving their time and talent through serving and active fundraising. And I thrived in the schools. By middle school, I was winning spelling bees, and in high school I was a member of multiple clubs and president of five. I was president of my class, and I won the senior award for having "done most for the school and most likely to succeed." I had also developed my love of science, regularly winning prizes at the science fairs, ultimately leading to my Doctor of Pharmacy degree at University of Southern California's (USC) School of Pharmacy.

While I was a doctoral student at USC, I met a young man who was studying for his Doctor of Chiropractic at University of California-Northridge: my future husband Riadh Fakhoury. He later shared with me that the minute he saw me walk in the door of the youth group meeting, he knew he would marry me. He finished his studies before I did and chose to start up his practice in Ocala, Florida, where his parents lived. Several years later, when it was time for Riadh to get married, he confided in his father that he was interested in marrying me. It took a couple years to convince me!

This is how Ocala became my home, too. After I completed my clinical residency training in Gainesville, I accepted a position as Clinical Coordinator at a local hospital, while I was pregnant with our first child, and I joined my first local service organization, the Junior League of Ocala, where I advocated for the Science Center.

And so, began my family life, my professional life, and my community and philanthropic life in Ocala. I was so lucky to have had loving parents, who had modeled for me how to live a life of hard work, civic engagement, and philanthropy. Over the next decades I never stopped learning about and contributing to the community.

Being president of my class when I completed Leadership Ocala, I was made a non-voting member of the Chamber of Commerce. Owing to my ability to bring in fifty new members during a membership competition, I was asked to join the Executive Committee as Vice President of Membership.

For four years, I was a voting member of the Chamber and was Chair for a year. During my tenure as Chair, Ocala Chamber received its first five-star accreditation, a ranking achieved by only twenty-four other US cities that year.

After the Chamber, I was happy to take on other leadership roles. I chaired for several campaigns and events and was honored at a special event in recognition for my fundraising for our local college's foundation. I was the first woman on the board of the Suntrust Bank (now Truist), and I served on the boards of many other organizations. I share all of this to say community involvement was part of my DNA.

Over those years, my family became deeply rooted in Ocala. My five children had all attended and prospered at local private and public schools, my husband had expanded his practice and had founded Vestech Partners, and I was fully engaged in the life of the community, while still practicing at the local hospital. I loved my All-America City, and my city loved me. Or so I thought.

☙•❧

In 2013, two Jewish lawyers from Gainesville reached out to me. They were enthusiastic advocates of Sister Cities, a program instituted by President Eisenhower, primarily for promoting cultural and commercial ties. But Eisenhower also saw Sister Cities as a citizen diplomacy initiative, and to that end, Gainesville already had several sister cities, including Qalqilya in Palestine. They invited me to travel as a delegate to visit Qalqilya.

The trip was wonderful! We met in the mayor's office, and for fun, I took a seat behind the mayor's desk. One of my fellow travelers snapped a photo that I posted on social media. I was excited to talk with the mayor about Ocala's opportunity to become a part of this worldwide organization by initiating a sister city relationship with Ramallah.

With all the paperwork in hand, I took the proposal to the mayor and City Council on November 14, 2014. That morning, negative remarks started to surface on social media. One friend alerted me about Facebook posts encouraging people to come to the meeting in opposition. Another got a message saying, "Some Muslim wanted to turn Ocala into a sister city with Ramallah. All Christians should show up."

I had arranged to take some guests, as well as a group of students in the youth version of Leadership Ocala, to the meeting. Aware of opposition, but still determined, we arrived with the proposal as planned. As the first two students began to speak, the mayor interrupted with "This is a mayor-to-mayor agreement." Then, he turned to an aide and said, "Put the photo up."

The photo was the one I had posted on my social media page: me at the desk of the mayor of Qalqilya. Behind me hung photos of Yasser Arafat and Mahmoud Abbas, the then-President and Prime Minister of Palestine, official photos of the country's leadership, just as you would find in any government office, whether it was in Palestine or the US.

The mayor then theatrically pointed to the photo, declaring, "I have a concern about Manal's relationship with these terrorists!" And the council room exploded into a babble of crazy, nasty voices from the crowd. My daughter Laila, who was part of the young Leadership group, was horrified. She burst out against the language the crowd was using about Palestinians. "Why are you talking about them like they are trash? They are people! There are kids, ice cream shops, taxi drivers!"

The council announced they wouldn't do the agreement. I was stunned. It was like an out-of-body experience. I didn't cry; I was simply numb. Later that evening, Laila was still appalled, exclaiming, "After everything you have done for this city, that is how they treat you?!" I wasn't Manal, former Chair of the Chamber of Commerce, Person of the Year, prominent cheerleader for the city. No, I was "a Muslim," and Muslims are scary. I was Palestinian and, thus, worthy of being dehumanized.

In the months following, letters appeared in the newspaper condemning the November council meeting and the mayor's behavior. But I had become detached. I stopped attending community events. Instead, I decided to reconsider where to spend my time and resources.

Then one afternoon, a serendipitous letter from an inmate at the Florida Department of Corrections arrived in the mail. It was a plea for me to come in and start a Gavel Club for the prisoners. A Gavel Club is a way to bring the Toastmasters' experience of personal development to groups who may be ineligible for regular membership. I invited my Toastmasters friends to join me at the prison. We quickly learned how fulfilling it was to serve this community. What started with just one unit soon spread throughout the facility, eventually leading to thirteen Gavel Clubs and a personal development program.

In December 2017, I had an epiphany: I could be doing so much more. I posted that I was looking for one hundred women to join me for a leadership project, though I didn't even know quite yet what that project was. My post nearly went viral, and I very quickly had my group of women. Our women's non-profit, Ollin Women International, formed almost effortlessly.

Realizing that many people in Ocala didn't know the difference between Palestine and Pakistan, we focused on getting people to understand basic principles: that we wanted to create, not destroy, and that the focus was not narrowly on Palestine but widely on peace-building. We wanted to designate Ocala as an International City of Peace.

We could make our own proposal to the global umbrella organization without having a City Hall endorsement. As a courtesy, though, we wanted to let City Hall know what we were doing.

For the first meeting, the mayor was not present, and we had an impressive number of influential women in the group. The council members, who were present, just fumbled with papers, saying they wanted more information.

The second time, the mayor was there. I was not the presenter, but halfway through the presentation, the mayor stopped the proceedings and said, "Whose idea is this? Dr. Fakhoury, is this your idea? Would you please stand up and address us?" I answered questions, but the Council still didn't give us a response.

We were asked to come back for a third time, but our group balked. "Why should we bother going back? We don't need to have the Council's okay." The proposal, however, remained on the agenda. At their next meeting, the Council decided that Ocala would be a City of Compassion, instead, because "Manal isn't qualified to speak about peace." And just as in 2014, the meeting dissolved into chaos, marked by threats to call police.

We continued our peace-building efforts on our own, and Ocala became a City of Peace. I continued my commitment to civic organizations. And I continued to feel that I could do even more to support the city I love, even in the face of prejudice and roadblocks among city leaders.

So, on July 1, 2021, I declared my intention to run for mayor against the incumbent.

I thought that Ocala was ready to have fresh leadership and a woman as mayor, and I knew I would work hard, raise money, and run a professional campaign. I felt that my long and proven track record of getting things done would hold up well against a career politician, who had achieved very little over the course of his five terms in office.

Yes, there were those who warned me that my opponent and his supporters would run a dirty campaign, but I was ready to forge through it. When my young campaign aide and I knocked on doors, we would be greeted with smiles and "Manal, you helped my son with his speech assignment" or "You were so instrumental in getting my problem solved." Some of these memories went back more than thirty years.

Even with strong support from super volunteers and Republicans and Democrats and the endorsement of the Black pastors, the PAC was undermining my campaign with a vicious fear-mongering crusade. They sent out reams of attack mailers with a string of lies: Manal wants to defund the police. Manal wants to open the borders. Manal wants to change our way of life. They made signs calling me a terrorist and claiming I was an advocate of Sharia law. Businesses were threatened if they posted my signs. Pseudo friends confessed that, yes, I was well respected and had done a lot, but they couldn't vote for me because I was Muslim.

Not once did my detractors talk with me about municipal policy or what my hopes were for the continued betterment of Ocala.

The day before the election, voices on the radio began to declare that I was going to win in a landslide. While normally this would be good news, instead, it acted as a dog whistle for the PAC and its supporters. The morning of the election, citizens in all nineteen precincts woke up to find their neighborhoods flooded with yard signs with only one graphic: against a white background my name Manal inside a red circle with a red slash across it. And cellphones lit up with photo texts to get out the vote because "our safety and quality of life depend on it."

I did not win the election. The turnout was the highest on record, but that wasn't the only extreme about the election. Our local gazette stated my race, faith, and involvment with some outside organizations were the subject of more political vitriol and fake news than ever experienced in Ocala's history.

I had thought my city was better than that. Instead, they took someone who had served the community for decades and had a strong track record and demonized and vilified her based on her faith and heritage.

The personal attacks did not stop, even when the election was over. The mayor continued to spread his lies at a Menorah lighting ceremony in November. A witness quoted in the *Ocala Gazette* shared that the mayor "actually came out and said that all the organizations that [Manal] works on are a front for Hamas."

Having to face these kinds of repeated underhanded tactics of smearing reputations and poisoning civic discourse is not new for Muslims, especially female Muslims. When the Sister Cities proposal was rejected, a friend commented that if he had made the proposal, it would have sailed right through—because he was a Jewish man. After the election, many people said that if I had been a blonde, Christian white woman, none of the negativity would have happened.

I have been asked, from time to time, how I survived the personal attacks, and I believe there are three reasons why I am able to continue with my message of communication, reconciliation, and healing. One reason is a uniquely American one: the ability for anyone in this country to "come back" time and time again. It is one of the most glorious things about our nation. I have found solace, as well, in so many locally, who were there tirelessly fighting for my campaign.

I also truly believe that there may be some good that comes out of all that happened to me. For one thing, it brought clearly to the surface the strain of bigotry and prejudice based on race and religion that lay beneath the all-American façade. Community voices have begun to push back. After the mayor's remarks at the Menorah lighting became widely known, other civic leaders came out to publicly denounce the mayor, including officers of the local NAACP chapter and the Bridges Project (which works to eliminate racial and social injustice), who appeared at a City Council meeting to read into the official record condemnations of the mayor's words and behavior.

Young people have been spurred into action as well. A senior high school student came to interview me after the election for a documentary he planned to submit for a competition. He called the documentary *Madame Mayor*. A student at the University of Florida contacted me about an article she was writing that she had hopes of placing with *The New York Times*.

As for me, I chose to take the high ground and did not stoop to retaliate with their ugly methods. Instead, just as I took on starting the Gavel Club after the Sister Cities attack and just as I went on to establish Ocala as a City of Peace after the mayor's insults, I have moved on from the election. I continue to serve on national boards and often have to turn down requests to serve on more boards. I field invitations and explore opportunities.

Ocala residents stop me to ask what I will do next. Some have suggested that I run for a state position. I don't know yet, but it is something to think about.

What I do know is that I will not apologize for being a female Palestinian Muslim. It is absolutely the best part of me. Rather than spreading fear and hate, I want to lead others to show that in America, the will to succeed is always welcomed here.

ABOUT THE AUTHOR

DR. MANAL FAKHOURY

For the past thirty-five years, Dr. Manal Fakhoury has been making a difference in Ocala with hard work, generosity, and outstanding leadership. She founded Ollin Women International, a women's foundation dedicated to creating a more compassionate and equitable society and is the curator and licensee holder for TEDxOcala, bringing the series of leadership and personal development talks to our community. Visit www.myfli.com or www.vestechpartners.com to learn more.

5

A TALE OF THREE HOSPITALS

by Sydney Rafferty

On March 13, 2020, I was raped. I got drunk with my friends and met a man—who turned out to be not so nice. But this story isn't about that. It's about the trauma I experienced from the people who were supposed to help me.

Mere months earlier, I had trained with the Alachua County Victims' Services and Rape Crisis Center helpline. I was now certified with the Florida Council Against Sexual Violence and had a comprehensive knowledge of Florida's laws and regulations about the administration of sexual assault examinations and what to do if you get raped. Through the hotline, I helped other women. I knew what to do. I knew the service providers weren't always easy to work with and that the whole situation could be overwhelming, but I thought it was nothing I couldn't handle.

☙•❧

The assault happened in Crystal River, Florida, in a different county from where I volunteered. My best friend Taylor drove me straight to the hospital for a rape kit. It was around 4:00 a.m. when we arrived. I went straight to the counter and requested a sexual assault exam. The woman looked annoyed but directed me to an intake room. After explaining the situation, the staff member asked if I wanted them to contact law enforcement. I wasn't sure if I wanted to report, so I just said, "Not yet."

Tired and still drunk, all I knew was I wanted them to collect the evidence from my body as soon as possible. I had to pee, but I was holding it. I knew the first urination after a rape was some of the most important evidence collected.

Once in the exam room, I requested a cup to collect my urine. They had allowed Taylor to come back with me. After a while, she crawled into the unwelcoming hospital bed with me, and we both rested.

A large police officer came bumbling into the room without warning. Confused and shocked, I explained what had happened when he asked me. He asked if I wanted to report the incident. I told him that I didn't, although I still wasn't sure. I thought maybe I was just making a big deal out of nothing.

I knew cops could be difficult to work with in these situations. I knew I might feel like he didn't believe me. I knew he might say some weird victim-blamey stuff, but I was not prepared for the level of bullshit I got.

"If you don't want to report the incident, you can look at this as a learning experience. Listen to your sober friends next time," the officer told me. I was speechless.

"I'm sorry, what?" I asked, daring him to dig himself deeper into a hole.

"Let me give you some advice," he haughtily continued. "The best way to avoid situations like this is self-control." I didn't know where to begin. He continued, "Yeah, you know, just not putting yourself in vulnerable situations."

I decided to drop it for the time being. He found out I volunteered with the rape crisis hotline, though, and it got worse. "You're a rape crisis counselor?" he asked.

"Yes," I answered curtly.

"So…you give people advice on this stuff, but…you can't…?" He trailed off, but I knew exactly what he meant. He was asking why I couldn't follow my own advice not to get raped. That's not even what we do on the hotline, but I knew better than to try to explain that to this insect of a man.

"What the fuck did you just say to me?" I was absolutely floored by the man's gall.

"Well, I'm just saying, you give people advice on this, but…" He couldn't seem to finish that thought.

"But what?" I prompted, ready for a fight.

"You know…" He was trying to play it off. He knew that I was upset, but he would never understand how unacceptable his words were.

At this point, I noticed that I had been in this hospital room for at least an hour without seeing a nurse. Half joking, I asked if I were ever going to get an exam. "Oh no, they don't do that here," replied the cop. "It's mostly old people around here, and old ladies don't get raped. If they do, they're mostly like 'woohoo I got some!'" I was done with this man.

When the nurse came back, I asked her when I would get my exam, but she just confirmed that they didn't do them. She said that only a specially certified nurse could do the exam, but that wasn't true. I couldn't believe it. Why did they put me in a room? I told her that she legally had to give me one, and all I got was a simple apology as she left. She said that I would have to go to Gainesville to get one, over an hour's car ride away. I knew my rights. This wasn't supposed to happen to me! This happened to people who didn't know their rights but not to me! I had done everything I was supposed to do. It hadn't mattered.

Taylor drove me back to her house. It was nearly 7:00 a.m., and I needed to rest before I could go back out into the world and try again.

Several hours later, I woke up feeling like garbage, but at the same time, surprisingly okay. Taylor gave me some fresh clothes to wear, and I set off for another day of fighting to receive basic health care.

I had been told to go to Gainesville for the exam, but there was a closer hospital in Ocala that should do the exams. I met my friend David, showed him the discharge paperwork from the previous hospital, and said that we needed to go to another one. He simply said, "Let's go."

I drove us to the sexual assault center in Ocala and parked in their lot, but I decided that I would call them before going in to possibly save some time and heartache. A woman answered the phone, confirmed they did do the exams, and asked if I had filed a report. I hadn't. "Okay," she said. "You're going to need to do that before we can administer the exam."

I was stunned. One of the first things I'd been taught in training was that you did not need to report the crime to receive medical attention. I was speaking to a certified rape crisis center. Why were they telling me this?

"No, actually, legally, I don't have to report to get the exam."

"Yes, you do," she said. There was just no arguing with that. Panic raced through me, as I started to worry I wouldn't be able to get my exam done anywhere. I centered myself and tried to continue the conversation.

"Okay, so if I do report, can I get an exam with you?"

"Well, we do have a specially certified nurse, but unfortunately, we won't be able to help you because the assault happened in another county," the woman responded.

"But, in the county it happened in they said that they couldn't help me!" I pleaded with her.

"I'm sorry, but you'll have to go back to the county where the rape happened to get a rape kit," she replied plainly.

I hung up, now frozen with panic and confusion. She had told me to go back to the county that just sent me away. A certified rape crisis center had told me this, basically this county's equivalent to where I volunteered and had done my training. How could this be happening? Was I embarking on a wild goose chase for simple medical care? Was anyone going to help me? I didn't know the answers to any of these questions, but I knew I had to keep trying.

We headed over to another hospital in Ocala. I was nervous that something similar may happen there, but it was right across the street, so why not? I needed to try. We walked into the emergency room and up to the front desk, and I asked for a sexual assault exam, just as I'd done at the first hospital.

After waiting a few minutes, I was escorted to a room. They began by taking my vitals, and I told them all about what had happened at the first hospital. I was still wearing the band. They acted shocked and appalled, saying that they would certainly get me what I needed. But then they told me they didn't actually do sexual assault exams there.

"What do you mean? You legally have to give me this exam," I said, cautious but insistent.

It was the same story about needing the specially certified nurse, and I—again—stated that any nurse can perform the exam. It didn't matter. They then said that they could call a specially certified nurse for me.

Okay, I thought. "So, you do do exams here..." I was suspicious. At this point, I didn't trust anyone. They brought me back to a room where I waited for around twenty minutes. I sat on the bed nervously, while David paced around the room, silent but clearly beginning to fume. When a doctor finally came in, I held my breath, waiting to hear what he would say. I tried to prepare myself for disappointment, but I couldn't help but hope.

"So we called our specialty nurse, and unfortunately—" My heart sank. "We can't help you." That was all David needed.

"What do you mean you can't help her?" he roared.

"Look, I'd really like to help y—," the doctor started, but David cut him off.

"No, okay, this is a victim of a crime sitting here in front of you, and you're telling me you can't help her?" I was a little embarrassed by how angry he was getting but also incredibly relieved to not feel so alone and be able to have someone in my corner.

"I'd really like to help you, but, legally I can't. You'll have to go back to the county where the assault occurred. We just don't have the jurisdiction." This is where I found my voice.

"The jurisdiction? No," I said, " medical jurisdiction isn't a thing. What do you mean you don't have the jurisdiction? What even is that?" I was at a loss for words. I was trying to keep it together and not let my emotions get the better of me, but I was slipping fast.

David continued yelling at the doctor and just being generally appalled, while I started to slip into a panic. The voices around me faded out, and I started to cry. I told the doctor that the Citrus County hospital turned me away, so I couldn't go back there. This doctor was the most empathetic person I had met so far, though, and he genuinely seemed like he wanted to help me. But he just said, "I'm sorry, I can't."

I asked to speak with their SANE nurse, and he told me that she wasn't there. He said they shared a SANE nurse with a few hospitals, and she was in a different county at the moment. They had spoken to her on the phone, and she had told them that she couldn't help me because of the jurisdiction. I still had tears silently running down my cheeks, when I asked them if they could at least give me the STI treatments that come with a sexual assault exam. They looked at me, confused, and looked at each other with hesitation. My patience had run thin at this point, so I didn't wait for them to give me whatever bullshit answer they were concocting.

"A sexual assault exam has three main components to it: making sure the victim is physically okay, collecting evidence, and treating them for STIs and pregnancy. I understand that you can't collect my evidence, but can you at least give me the STI and pregnancy treatments?" I had done my speech about what a sexual assault exam was and what happens in it enough times while volunteering that I was able to spit that out fluently. The doctor seemed to understand and said, "Yeah, yeah, I can give you those treatments."

"Yes. I know you can." I was infuriated. Medical jurisdiction? I stared at them, daring them to give me any more fuel for my anger. They dared not. I can only imagine how I must've looked—heartbroken, enraged, determined. They left the room. I let out a giant sigh and decided it was time to call the Alachua County Victims' Services staff member on call. She was horrified, and it felt so validating. I confirmed with her that if I went to the hospital in Gainesville, they would help me, even though the assault happened in a different county. She told me that she was certain I could get a full rape kit done there and told me that she would meet me there if I wanted, to make sure everything went smoothly.

The doctor came back in with a prescription for HIV prophylaxis and said that he could at least offer me that. I took it, thanked him, and told him that I was leaving to go to Gainesville. He tried to stop me, saying he could do something for me. Maybe he was trying to get me to sign something, but I was too upset, and David was done. He gave everyone hell as we left, saying that they should be ashamed to call themselves a hospital, if they wouldn't help a victim in need. I was embarrassed but couldn't find it in myself to disagree. He was a giant shield, protecting me as he led me out of the hospital battlefield. We got to my car, and he offered to drive to the hospital in Gainesville. I eagerly accepted.

I was a mess, and I wasn't sure I even wanted to go to a third hospital. Even though I had been assured that I would be able to get an exam there, I was out of hope and unsure if I could handle another rejection.

I thought that maybe I hadn't actually been raped. I thought that, surely, if I'd actually been raped, this wouldn't be happening. Right? *Right*? I didn't know what to think anymore. The way David called me the "victim of a crime" before in the hospital—it hit different. It made me realize the gravity of my situation but also made me question if it really was that serious. Was I just making a big deal out of nothing? I thought about all these things as David drove us the hour to Gainesville.

The drive felt simultaneously too long and too short. When I saw the advocate from the rape crisis center there, I immediately felt relief. We went to the counter and asked for an exam, and I—finally—was given one. I decided I would report the assault with the Gainesville Police Department, which would then forward it to the Citrus County Sheriff's Office.

I had to answer some awkward questions. I described the rape and stated, "He fucked me." The officer asked me to describe exactly what I meant by that. I didn't know what to say, so I went with the basics: "He put his penis in my vagina and moved it in and out repeatedly." What else was I supposed to say to that?

It was about twenty-two hours after the assault occurred, valuable time when considering evidence collection. That made me angry, but I knew that I did the best that I could. I was grateful for my privilege in this situation. Not everyone would've been able to drive to Gainesville from Citrus County. It made me angry to think about the people in my situation, who couldn't drive that distance to get an exam. I was still confused and enraged, but I could finally feel some peace now that my exam was done. The medications made me ill, so David drove me to his home, where he cared for me through the next day.

Weeks later, I received a call from my dad asking about some hospital bills. I hadn't told him what had happened, and I really didn't want to. I simply told him not to pay the bills. He didn't understand, but he accepted I wasn't ready to share what had happened yet. Sexual assault exams are free, yet both of the hospitals in Crystal River and Ocala had sent me a bill for visiting their emergency rooms. It's true that I didn't receive an exam at either one of those places, but I certainly didn't feel that a bill was warranted. I called them both to explain the situation, and they bascially told me to buzz off. I felt like I was being extorted. I contacted the Florida Bar, the Agency for Health Care Administration, the Florida Council Against Sexual Violence—anyone I could think of to help me, but to no avail.

Finally, I made the decision to make a TikTok video quickly describing what had happened. I posted it on TikTok, but more importantly, I posted it on Instagram and Facebook and tagged the hospitals. Within hours I was overwhelmed with support. People were sharing my post! They were angry with and for me. It felt good and validating. Later that day, I received messages from both hospitals saying they would retract the bills. I was still beyond angry.

I knew that there was much work left to be done to make sure this never happened to anyone again, but I felt empowered by my anger, empowered by the many people standing behind me, eager to help. I knew that this was only the beginning, but I felt so ready to take on the challenge.

ABOUT THE AUTHOR

SYDNEY RAFFERTY

Sydney Rafferty is a twenty-five-year-old graduate of the University of Florida. She got her bachelors degree in psychology and plans to return to school to earn a doctorate in clinical psychology. After college, she worked in child protective investigations in Gainesville, Florida, before moving to Orlando, Florida. Sydney is a theatre lover and performs whenever she can, and she especially loves to use the arts to better the world, like this book is doing.

6

THE BULLY WHO GOT BETTER

by Jacqueline Korpela

My first experiences with abuse, shame, and bullying mostly occurred at school and my home, the two places that a kid should feel the most protected. My father bullied my mother, who took out her frustration on my older brother. My brother passed his abuse unto us, and we, in turn, bullied each other. When I had issues with bullying in school, I wouldn't confide in my family, because I knew I wouldn't be protected. I never developed the tough outer skin that some do; instead, I have always internalized others' views of myself and masked so hard to fit in. I took the idea of "treat people how you want to be treated" to an extreme. I grew into a people-pleaser, trying to be kind and helpful to avoid conflict. I thought I was coping. I was not. I was barely surviving. I needed Broke Bitches Psychotherapy.

Some call it Shadow Work, the unlearning of harmful coping mechanisms, the learning & disabling of my triggers, and the building of a foundation of skills that would help me thrive. But I like Broke Bitch because our healthcare system is a joke. I've fallen between the cracks of medical care so often, I cobbled together my own tools for healing myself over the years. I needed therapy for the trauma I endured as a child—trauma that I had to revisit and work through to come out the other side, as a healthy, growing adult.

I will start by talking about bullying in school and transition to my home life. The people-pleaser in me is so nervous to share my childhood and acknowledge abuse that I called by so many names before admitting what it was. Even as I write this, my hands sweat and my throat feels tight, thinking about my family's reactions when reading this.

Sitting on the bleachers of my middle school, I was approached by a girl, who had been sitting with a group of girls. I looked up from my book and smiled at her. I didn't know her personally, but I had seen her around school.

"Do you even shower?" she demanded. "Your hair is oily, and you stink!" She laughed, smugly satisfied with herself.

My blood felt like ice in my veins; my face grew red and hot. I murmured, "Of course..." But the girl was already walking back towards her friends, who were giggling at her boldness.

I scooped up my stuff and retreated to the bathroom to cry it out before classes started. I have thought about that conversation so many times over the years. I envisioned smacking her across the face, saying something equally as cruel, or even just giving her my honest response to her question. Maybe it would have stopped her in her tracks and made her consider that she doesn't know everyone's story. Maybe she would have laughed harder.

The fact was that I was part of a big family living in poverty. There were occasions when we would live without electricity for an extended amount of time. I hate cold water, and I struggle to breathe comfortably in it. Other than the occasional angel friend offering our big family use of their shower for the night, my choices were a cold shower that felt like torture or skipping a day or so.

I didn't let them see me cry. I refused to give them the satisfaction. I got up and left the bleachers. It took everything I had to hold it together until I was out of sight.

Again in middle school, a boy set his sights on me and asked me if I would be his girlfriend. He gave me a necklace, and we would hold hands some. It started super innocent, which was great for me because I was inexperienced. I don't think he even ever kissed me, but he got it into his head that he was allowed to start groping me. He grabbed me between the legs a few times during PE class. I gave him back his necklace and told him that I was not okay with his touching and that I didn't want to get to know him any better.

He laughed in my face, pulled my shirt open, and dropped the necklace into my bra. He declared, "I don't care, and I will touch you wherever I want."

Some girls from my homeroom found me crying in the bathroom, and I confided in them about the situation. They told me that I had to report it. I fought them so hard on it.

Eventually, I did make a report, and the way it was handled makes me so angry to this day. My parents were never informed about the incident or that I had met with the principal. The principal called in the boy and sat with us at the table. She had us both give our account of the events and had the boy read the page on sexual harassment in the code book. That was it. I still had to attend classes with him and deal with him staring daggers at me. He spit in my face from the school bus as I was walking by once. I didn't even tell that time, because I felt sure nothing would come of it.

My saving grace was the library, I would finish early in almost every class and then volunteer there. We were switching from the old card and stamp system to the new barcode system. The ladies that worked there were so helpful and kind. One of them gave me some hand-me-down clothing from her daughter. It was the one place in that school where I felt safe.

Why didn't I tell my parents what happened at school? It could have been because I didn't think they would have believed me or that they wouldn't have done anything about it, even if they did.

☙•☙

When I think about it, my first experiences with bullying and shame started at home. I grew up hearing my parents being incredibly disrespectful to each other. My father would say petty and cruel things to my mother, and she would retaliate in kind. There were personal jabs, and there were things my dad would say about lusting over other women that neither my mother nor we children ever should have had to hear. My siblings and I mimicked what we saw and were openly disrespectful to each other.

Everyone had a weakness to exploit, and therefore, no one was safe. My youngest sister K had a birthmark on her lower back that we never missed a chance to tell her it looked like a poop stain. We also convinced her once that she was adopted. The sister closest to me in age would be teased about her flat chest, and we called her "Five Head" to make her insecure about her forehead. I was made fun of most for my body hair and weight, which would have been wrong no matter what.

It hurts to look back and realize I internalized their criticisms and believed them true when they weren't at all. Eventually, as I turned to food for comfort, it became a self-fulfilling prophecy.

J, my oldest brother, was the most abusive of all, and I believe it was his harassment that caused each of us to pick on one another. He was the oldest and should have been the example, but to this day, he is still one of the cruelest people I know. His abuse wasn't only verbal: It was also physical, and it was constant. He sexually abused me and laughed in my face when my dad didn't believe me. "Dad took me fishing and told me what you said. He believes me, not you. Thanks for the candy and the fishing trip." He would hold me down and let his spit linger in a long line close to my face. When he felt benevolent, he would suck it back up before it made contact. Most times, I would end up with a face full of spit.

When our fights turned physical, our parents would tell us to beat the hell out of each other in another room, so as not to bother them.

It was bad enough being the butt of fat jokes from my sister and brother, but it was so much worse to hear it from my father. I was twelve, reading my book on the couch. My father was sitting on the ground, in front of the couch, watching TV with my brother. My younger sister walked in front of the television, and my dad chastised her for blocking it. Then, without missing a beat, he told me, "Jackie, you are blocking the living room."

This same man now tells me, "How do you not know how beautiful you are?"

Shameless 49

When I remind him about that incident, he laughs at his wit and claims it was all in good fun. The lapse in his reasoning astounds me.

Recently, I heard my father was teasing my sister about gaining weight. My sister has a mental illness that keeps her from working, and she has to live at home with my parents. At her worst, she had lost so much weight, I was sure she was dying. She was finally prescribed meds that have given her enough normalcy that we can sometimes hold phone conversations. It has been such a blessing, so hearing that my father dared to tease her about weight gain—which was a side effect of her finally being properly medicated—made me see red. My mom told me about this but asked me not to tell him she said anything. If my dad knows that Mom told on him, he would take it out on her.

I wanted to be clever about calling him out, so he wouldn't know I was covering for my mom. I am already the weird rainbow black sheep of my family, so I told him that I was meditating and that my guides gave me a message for him. I told him they reminded me about how he treated me about my weight my whole life, and they revealed to me that he was verbally abusing K over her weight, as well. I told him that they asked me to talk to him and request that he use compassion with my sister. I explained how his words still echo in my head and affect me as an adult. I told him that his jokes could cause his other daughter to stop medicating and possibly become violent again. He heard me out and didn't turn angry. I have no idea and little hope that he will change his behavior, but I was proud of myself for finding a way to talk to him. At least, he was willing to hear me out.

I wonder, sometimes, how my parents' experience with shame and bullying shaped them as people. My dad didn't have a father, and his mother modeled much of the same behavior. We hated visiting her. That might sound mean, but the last time I saw that woman, she straight up told my sister she was too thin, I was too fat, and that I should give some of my fat to my smaller sister.

Thinking about my dad having that woman as a mother, I can better understand why he has such a warped view of women. My dad will tell you he loves women, but he only loves to look. He loves the idea of them. In theory, they are wonderful, but in reality, he wonders why they have to be real people with emotions. Why can't they just look nice and be pleasant all of the time?

My mother wouldn't name call or outright fat shame. She would bully herself in front of us. She hated her fat body and could never leave the house "without her face on." I didn't know my mom was fat; she was just my mom. I thought she was beautiful. She didn't feel beautiful, though. Motherhood left her carrying more weight than she was used to, and she was married to a lech, who never stopped checking out women and commenting on their looks.

My aunt wasn't much better. She and my mother would talk to me about my body, exclaiming that I was doomed for having cellulite on my legs at such a young age. "You can never get rid of that!" They made me feel like I was starting at a deficit because of some adorable little dimples on my thighs.

I do self-love exercises, now, to try to love my curves and dimples. I mourn how much time I lost hating my own body, hating all the parts that play on lights and shadows. It wasn't until I could find a way to love my body where it was that I cared enough to get any healthier. The more shame I felt, the more I abused myself in a sad cycle of self-hate. My claiming to be healthy doesn't mean that I got skinny. It means that I stopped punishing myself over food or numbers on a scale. I no longer eat out of depression or boredom, and I no longer exercise as punishment. I love fresh and healthy food. I also like junk food. I have learned about balance and listening to my body.

I found a type of exercise that I love. Moving my body is no longer a punishment but a pleasure! When I look at my body now, I see strength and power. I thank it for all it does for me. The endorphins I get from skating make me feel incredible. I coach a local roller derby team, and in them, I have found a group of women who are warriors like me. We breathe life into each other and help break up old ways of thinking that hold us back.

I think a major turning point in my healing was moving four hours away from home. I enjoyed the space from my birth family. I didn't feel close to any of them, and dealing with them stressed me out. Over the years, I have worked on developing a relationship with my blood family that is more authentic and loving. We have had ups and downs, and sometimes, we went without contact for long periods of time, while I was processing things.

How did I reconcile how I was treated as a child and decide what my relationship with my parents would look like once I left their home? First, I understand that my parents are humans that were a result of their treatment and experiences growing up. They didn't have access to resources and information like we do today. I set very clear boundaries. I take time off when I need it. I also unapologetically recall memories and talk through them with my parents and siblings, so I can work through them myself. I recognize it's my job to heal myself and decide what my relationship with my parents and siblings should look like.

Over the years, my siblings and I—minus my oldest brother, who never learned to take responsibility or heal through things—have talked about how we were raised and what we would change. I have apologized for the part I played in handing down emotional and verbal abuse, instead of letting it end with me. I have told my siblings that I regret the time we lost fighting and hating, when we could have been a support to each other. I try to be a safe person for them to confide in, and I am vocal about what our relationship means to me.

Am I over it all? No. I think it's a lifelong journey of self-love. Saying kind things to myself can still feel silly and forced, but I am learning. Sometimes, it means telling that mean voice in my head to shut up. Sometimes, it is repeating affirmations until they stop sounding silly and start sounding like truth. I try to examine my relationship to food and dieting, be honest about my disordered eating, and make sustainable changes. I set strong boundaries with my personal relationships and stand up for myself when I am being treated unfairly. I learned long ago that no one is going to save me but myself.

Reading *The Four Agreements: A Practical Guide to Personal Freedom* by Don Miguel Ruiz helped me gain perspective, especially when it comes to being authentic with my words and not taking anything personally. The verbal abuse I grew up with isn't a reflection of myself, but a reflection of those that experienced abuse and just passed it on.

As an adult, I have made a conscious decision to do better, to not only not harm, but to try to heal with my words. As a parent, I have always treated my children with respect and autonomy. I never speak down to them, and I apologize when I make mistakes. I have never allowed my children to be ugly to each other or hit one another. They disagree at times, but they have the tools to communicate without saying hurtful things. It has been so healing for me to create the home atmosphere that I always wished I'd had myself. I feel like I am healing my own inner child by raising my kids this way.

ABOUT THE AUTHOR

JACQUELINE KORPELA

Jacqueline (Jackie) Korpela is a homemaker in Central Florida and mother of six children and partner to David and Stephanie. She is a photographer with Starry Eyes Photography. Her birth photography is featured in the *Beautiful Births* documentary. Jackie considers herself a professional muse and "Jackie Of All Trades." In her free time, she is Haley's Vomit, coach for the Ocala Cannibals Roller Derby team.

SECTION TWO

Shattered but Not Broken

7

GROWING THROUGH THE REARVIEW MIRROR

by Lauren Debick

My head was propped in my hand as I watched the white lines of the highway blur by the car window. The temperature was comfortable inside my red 2014 Ford Escape, and Christmas music was gently playing over soft snoring coming from the backseat. I glanced over at my husband who was drumming his fingers on the wheel and humming along to the music that was playing on the radio. It was the middle of the night, and we were almost twelve hours into our twenty-hour road trip to see my family in Cleveland, Ohio for Christmas. I continued looking around the car and saw the Diet Coke stain above me from when my mom's bottle of pop exploded all those years ago. In that moment, I realized how the person riding in the same car, driving along the same stretch of highway, making the same trip to Cleveland around the same time of year had changed so much.

I had gone through an awkward growth period early on in life but was also someone who excelled academically, had a good group of friends, supportive parents, and for the most part, knew who I was, what I wanted out of life, and how to get it. When I first moved to Central Florida in 2010, though, so much of that changed. I quickly found myself in a situation where I was away from friends and family, in an area not quite suited for me, doing work that was extremely unfulfilling. In those first few years I lived in Florida, so much of my identity was being challenged daily. I quickly found myself in a situation in which I was feeling depressed and unsure of what my next step would be. It was during this time I found myself in a relationship that I thought would be the answer to the question of who I was. In retrospect, one could argue this relationship did accomplish that because in getting out of that emotionally abusive relationship and learning all the lessons I did, it has helped me become the person I am today.

Henry and I worked together, and I was drawn to him because he was someone who seemed to be successful, had a charming personality, and appeared to know what he wanted out of life. Most importantly, he took an interest in me at a time when I was feeling lost and unsure of where I was going. His eyes were the color of chocolate, he had dark hair that curled at the ends if he didn't keep it cut, and he could light a room up with his smile. He was shy in a way, but that shyness had me even more intrigued about who he was and what he was thinking at any given moment. In a way, he became my knight in shining armor as one of the first exchanges we had, he jumped my car for me when it died in the parking lot. We began texting and meeting one another for lunch, and it was during those initial conversations I found out he was new to the area, had a thirteen-year-old son whom he had full custody of, and he enjoyed sports and music.

Most of our conversations were done over text or in-person at the office. Looking back now, there were warning signs early on that I should have paid attention to, like the fact that, from week to week, his the tone and attitude toward our relationship changed. One day, everything was great and we would spend the night together, and the next day I wouldn't hear from him. That would lead to discussions about how this was not what he really wanted. I would ignore those things he said, because they were followed by invitations to come over and to go on dates with him.

This dance went on and on for months. Prior to my moving in with him, we had already "broken up" a handful of times. And yet, I continued to respond to him and be there for him when he reached out and said that he missed me. I liked the sweet words Henry would send me and the promises he would make about what our future could look like together, like camping and buying a log cabin in the mountains.

Emotional abuse is tricky, because it tends to be more subtle and covert compared to other types of abuse. My experience with this emotionally abusive relationship put me in a position where my self-esteem and confidence were chipped away, bit by bit, until I felt like there was only the shell of myself left. There are various signs someone may be in an emotionally abusive relationship, and in my case, the strongest signs were that of chaos and stonewalling. Stonewalling is when a person shuts down and closes themselves off from someone else because they are feeling overwhelmed or flooded with emotions that they are not able to manage. Stonewalling, in essence, is when a person builds a wall between them and their partner. Henry was stonewalling me from very early on in the relationship.

I moved in around the same time he was getting frustrated with his work situation and was looking at entrepreneurial options he was interested in and wanted me to be a part of. I set out to make the house a home for us. We worked together on redecorating and rearranging the spare bedroom to be made into an office for the business we were building together. We spent evenings watching movies and the weekends at Disney World. He even convinced me to buy a new car for the "family" so that we could have another vehicle to pull the camper. On the outside, it appeared we were heading in the direction of spending the rest of our lives together. On the inside, though, it was a very different story.

The first time my world was shattered in this relationship was when six months after I moved in, Henry walked into the office we shared and said, "I can't do this anymore. You have to move out." Both of us had left our jobs to start our business, and things were taking a while to get started. I had also enrolled in grad school, because I was looking for ways to get back to doing things I enjoyed and that made me feel like me. Education has always been important to me and starting the path to get my master's degree felt right. So much of who I was becoming was engulfed in the life we were creating: running the business, cooking, taking care of the house, and taking care of his son. While I was looking for stability and routine, I was also looking for him to recognize and love me for who I was and not just the things I was doing for him and his family and our business.

I tried to talk with him and convince him that we could make this work, but he spiraled into how he couldn't be what I wanted, and someday, I would want something more than he could give. All the while, I resisted and resisted and said we could make it work. After a week of false hope and being told maybe we can make this work, he came back to me and said, "No, you need to leave."

My mother flew down from Ohio on a Thursday morning to get directly into my car with me and drive back across the country she had just flown over. It was during this drive the Diet Coke explosion occurred. While I was so thankful for everything she had done for me, that did not take away from the pain I felt. By the time I got back to my mom's house in Ohio, I thought I was going to wither away and die. I spent a month on my mom's couch, barely eating or drinking or even moving.

My family and friends thought the worst of Henry and were glad to see me away from him. I, on the other hand, wanted nothing more than to be with him again. I missed the life we had created together and the stability and routine I thought were part of our relationship. In the back of my mind, the hope of us getting back together would creep in. He always came back, and I held on to the notion that he would come back to me again.

It took about one week of me being a thousand miles away for the texts to start up: "I miss you." "I am sorry." "I don't know why I said those things; I didn't really mean it." Every time I would get a text, my heart would race, and I would think this is it, he is going to say he was wrong and ask me to come back. Looking back, Henry never did say those exact words. What he did say was "I should get on a plane and fly up and get you and bring you back." But he never did. Instead, I took the bait and said that I would come back, and we could try to make it work again and the response was "Okay." That "okay" was all I needed; I had my car packed within twenty-four hours and was on my way across the country to Florida. A small voice in the back of my mind was trying to offer a warning, but I did not listen. My entire world had collapsed, and here I was, heading right back into the sinkhole that initiated the destruction.

When I got back, things were much better, for a bit, but then the stonewalling kicked in, again. It started with periods of silence, even though I tried to get Henry to tell me what was going on. My graduate program was in Communications, and it was absolutely infuriating to be writing papers and doing projects on effective and efficient communication when, inside my house and business, I could barely get Henry to look at me—let alone talk to me. I constantly felt like I was walking on eggshells and was in a state of waiting for the rug to be pulled out from under me. Sure enough, six months later and a few days before Christmas, a fight ensued that ended with the same words of "This isn't working. I can't do this anymore."

Instead of fighting and pleading and begging, this time, I left. I packed a few bags, grabbed my cat Marley, and got in my car to begin the one thousand-mile trek back to Ohio. At this point, I was furious. I had given myself completely to this man and his son and our business, and again, I was being pushed out and pushed away. This time, I went to my dad's house outside Cleveland with the intention of figuring out what the hell I was going to do in the new year.

During those next few weeks, I spent some time in Charleston, South Carolina with my cousin and went on several job interviews. Henry continued to text me and try to entice me to come back by telling me that things could be different and what happened before wasn't how he actually felt. I was so close to making the break and starting a new life far away from him and the pain and damage he had caused, but instead, I went back. I told him that if I came back, it would be for good. We would get married, and I would get a different job because running a business together was a constant source of stress. I drove back up to Ohio from South Carolina, picked up my things and Marley and turned around to drive back across the country, back to Florida, back to him.

At this point, my friends and family seemed to be in agreement that I was going to do what I wanted to do, no matter what kind of advice they gave. Henry told me over and over that what he said when he ended things was not really what he meant and not what he wanted. I was in such a fragile state emotionally, I would have done anything for him, never mind how detrimental it was to me.

I returned to him, and it is no surprise that things fell back into the same routine. I did not feel appreciated, supported, understood, or even loved. With the help of my friends and family, I started to realize I was worth so much more. The confidence I had in myself was growing, and while the stonewalling continued, I refused to plead and try to be what I thought he wanted me to be.

I remember waking up to a text from my dad sent a few days before Christmas, that my grandfather in Ohio had passed away the night before. I immediately went into making plans to go north for the funeral. I asked Henry if he wanted to come, and he said no. He rarely went to family functions with me, so this was no surprise. This time, it hit me differently. I have a vivid memory of walking into the church with my family the day of the funeral and looking over to the family section and seeing my sibling's and cousin's significant others and a wave of fury hit me. "He should be here with me," I thought, as tears rolled down my face.

When I came back from the funeral, I felt different. I felt as though a veil had been lifted from my eyes, and I could see what was right in front of me, clearly, for the first time in years. Being back home with my friends and family, who loved me and knew how to show love, provided that extra push I needed to stand up for myself. I finally knew what love looked like, and this relationship was not it. I told Henry I deserved better. I told him I deserved to be with someone who appreciated me, someone who supported me, someone who could communicate openly and truthfully with me, and someone who would love me for me. I am forever grateful to the friends and family that supported me in the days, weeks, and months that followed when I headed out on my own. While I had numerous breakdowns in the grocery store and many sleepless nights, I knew what I was doing was for the best.

Five years in the grand scheme of a lifetime is not that long, but in those five years, I became the truest version of myself. After I left, I eventually started a relationship with someone who truly appreciated me for who I was. This was the man that I would marry, and we would create a wonderful life together in which we respected one another, would say what we felt—as uncomfortable as it may be—and were understanding of who the other person was and what they needed to feel fulfilled.

While the experience of my early days in Florida presented me with some of my lowest moments, it also gave me the opportunity to find what was most important to me. My coping mechanisms throughout those years included writing, going to the beach, working on my spirituality, spending time with my pets, and giving my all to my graduate program.

I have become a woman who leans into my passions and tries new things, which has helped me become more confident. This isn't something that happened overnight; it took years of taking small steps in a new direction to become the truest version of myself. For so long, I feared being alone, which is the primary reason I kept going back. But then I realized that I had been alone all along (emotionally) and still found a way to persevere. If I could do that, what else could I do?

I have also become someone who fully believes in the power of forgiveness and gratitude. I forgave Henry a long time ago for all I went through. I was not in a position to make decisions that were best for me because of the emotional abuse I was going through, but that is not something I hold on to. Instead, I reflect on how grateful I am that this situation led me to the place I am now. I am so thankful for those who were there for me in the darkest moments, who listened to me, who let me cry on their shoulder, and who let me stay with them when I did not know where I was going to go. Having a strong support system is extremely important, both in good times and bad, and I am very grateful for my rocks that were there to hold me up when I felt like I was falling.

In my darkest of days, the light was found in my dreams, but it was that glimmer of hope I needed to keep me going. In the end, I came out on the other side of this situation with a positive attitude, a new perspective, more confidence, and a 2014 Ford Escape that will always remind me of where I have been and help me get to where I am going next.

ABOUT THE AUTHOR

LAUREN DEBICK

Lauren Debick is the creator and host of the Graceful Confidence Podcast and founder of Life Coaching with Lauren. She has a passion to serve as a source of light for those seeking inspiration, help, or advice, and strives to empower others to make choices that help them live their best life. She is a certified life coach and executive coach and has her accreditation in public relations. Lauren is actively involved in her community and enjoys spending time with her husband Andrew and her two step-sons. Visit **www.laurendebick.com** to learn more.

8

WHERE THE REAL POWER IS

by Katerina Mackenzie

"If you decide not to go through with it tomorrow, that's okay." my lawyer said. Her voice was calm and reassuring, and I wondered if the image I had of her in my mind's eye and the reality of her were at all similar. It was October 8, 2020, and because the world had not yet reached the peak of the COVID pandemic, I had never actually met with her in person. She had taken my case in June, pro-bono, and after an unsuccessful bid for dismissal by the defendant in July, the hearing was postponed until October 9th. I sat in a hammock chair on the balcony of the apartment I had moved into immediately following what has lovingly been nicknamed "Operation GTFO" and took a deep breath. It was the first truly autumnal evening of the season, and the chill in the breeze paired perfectly with the sense of dread steadily growing in the pit of my stomach. I thanked her for her patience with me and told her that I would be awaiting her call before our scheduled hearing-by-phone in the morning. After we hung up, I swayed slowly in the chair, my feet barely touching the floor, and the reality of my situation once again washed over me like a rogue wave.

The case that was to be decided the following day was concerning a restraining order against a man whose consistent and increasingly violent abuse over the course of our five-year relationship had pushed me to the brink of suicide. When I escaped the relationship in May 2020, he turned to stalking, going so far as to spend upwards of eight hours at the airport on the day he believed I was to return to Portland from visiting my family in Florida. He also took it upon himself to walk into the auto shop, where my car was being stored, to inquire as to whether or not it had been picked up. The months between receiving the initial restraining order and that moment were spent on a rollercoaster of legal proceedings, establishing and maintaining physical safety, constant hypervigilance, and the internal dissonance caused by knowing that I had support but still, at times, feeling utterly alone in the wake of this overwhelming experience.

It is common knowledge that abusers will isolate their victims, but what no one talks about is the isolation that comes with survival. Recovery from a violent relationship is so deeply traumatic and deeply personal that there are some aspects that can never be fully understood by others. On that evening, much of the difficult and dirty work of healing was still ahead of me. I wondered what would happen if I chose not to show up in the morning out of fear and, by extension, allowed the order to be dismissed. Would I be safe? Would my family, who was also included in the order, be safe? Would letting him get away with no legal repercussions finally placate him enough to make this stop?

I had no solid answers. All I had was years of experience living with a man who would stop at nothing to protect his image and his ego. These court proceedings had seriously wounded both, and I did not trust him for a moment not to take his pain out on those I loved most, if he could not get to me. The prospect of speaking my truth before a court of law and being cross-examined by a lawyer, who can best be described as a knock-off Bond villain, was terrifying, but the thought of him being allowed to hurt someone else because I did not speak up was far worse.

When the chill in the air finally became too much, I quietly padded back inside. The bedroom I now shared only with my beloved cat and dog was sparse but comfortable and slowly beginning to feel like home. This new life was a far cry from the squalor in which we had lived the last several years, and the adjustment was ongoing. After years of filth, shadiness, and secrecy, living in a clean space and environment that did not require secrecy or shame felt almost too good to be true. I settled into my bed and was soon joined by Alfred the tuxedo cat. He took his usual place on the pillow next to my head and purred contentedly. I reached up to scratch his ears, and he pressed his warm cheek into my hand. I wondered if he remembered being thrown across the room in a fit of anger by the man I was now seeking legal protection from. The same man who was now demanding that I give him the cat he was so quick to harm for no reason other than control. His blissful ignorance of the entire ordeal had proven to be a welcome reprieve from my constant awareness of it.

The negotiations between parties through our respective representatives had begun after the first hearing in July, and his lawyer, in lieu of actual negotiation skills, had opted instead to become progressively more belligerent and condescending with each interaction. My lawyer was Kathryn, a seasoned veteran of domestic violence cases, and she was having none of it. Her confidence in the face of harassment barely disguised as legal discourse gave me hope that all of his bluster and bravado could not drown out the truth. Despite all of her expert legal maneuvering and practicing of testimony with me, I still felt totally unprepared to testify and be cross-examined. I had told my story over and over again until I could do so without being overwhelmed with emotion. I detailed how he had abused and raped me, how he had both covertly and overtly threatened me, and how I was afraid for my safety. I was as prepared as I could be, but knowing that someone would be given the opportunity to question some of the most horrific experiences of my life on the record put a persistent knot in the pit of my stomach.

The morning I had anticipated and feared finally arrived. I clutched my cold brew and watched the clock slowly tick a minute past our scheduled start time, then two, and at the five minute mark, I took it upon myself to text Kathryn. "The court is just running a little late" she replied. "I'll call you when we're ready." After several more excruciatingly long minutes, the phone rang, and our hearing began. The judge, a polite but no-nonsense man, who had insisted on keeping the case on his bench since the first hearing in July, greeted everyone and explained the standard operating procedure of a hearing. "Do we all understand?" he asked after his brief explanation.

"Yes, Your Honor," I replied. There was a moment of silence.

"Mr. Pitfield, do you understand?" the judge inquired.

"Yeah," scoffed a voice that reverberated through my spinning brain like a gunshot. I knew he had been present, but hearing that voice again brought forth a flood of emotions that, while valid, I knew would not serve me in that moment. I did my best to ground myself before my time to speak.

As the party requesting the legal action, Kathryn and I would present our case first, which included my testimony, along with testimony from two others who had directly interacted with him in different capacities. The respondent, Andrew and his attorney, would then be allowed to cross-examine the witnesses before presenting their own case.

Kathryn called me to the stand and I took a deep breath before answering our practiced questions with a slight tremble in my voice. "No further questions, Your Honor," she said.

My chest tightened. It was time to face cross-examination by a man who was being paid by my abuser to discredit me in any way he could. I straightened my back against the chair, closed my eyes, and silently braced for impact.

The first question was wildly out of the scope of the hearing and, as such, was unceremoniously cut off and redirected by the judge before I could answer. It was at that moment that I realized that Andrew's attorney had built his case almost entirely on straw man arguments, what-ifs, and standard garden variety misogyny. He quickly refocused and began a line of questioning concerning a text message thread in which Andrew had threatened me. His intent was to try and make me say that this threat could have been misinterpreted, that I was overreacting and misreading. He repeated several variations of "Miss Mackenzie, what if he had said it to someone else?"

After the third iteration of the same irrelevant question, I lost my patience and found my voice. "He didn't say it to someone else. He said it to me!" I silently dared him to ask again.

"You've made your point. Move on, Counsel," the judge said curtly.

His final questions concerned the rape. His line of questioning was exactly what Kathryn and I had expected, albeit delivered much more crudely. I thought my blood would boil if I were presented with questions like "Did you say no?" and "Were you really afraid?" but I soon realized that a requirement for those questions to truly hurt would be respect for the person asking them. Upon realizing that I was a stone he could not draw blood from, I was allowed to step down. My part was over. I had spoken my truth, and now all I could do was listen, trust those who had shown up for me to do the same, and hope that was enough.

The two people who stepped up to testify on my behalf, one a near stranger and the other a beloved, lifelong friend, were both met with the same gentle confidence from Kathryn and bombastic swagger from the opposing attorney as I had been. Their unshakeable composure and grace under relentless pressure were inspiring. Win, lose, or draw, I could not have been more grateful for them. When the last witness was allowed to step down, it was time for the respondent to plead his case.

Andrew was called to the stand and sworn in. His attorney then led him through a series of questions about our relationship, the timeline of the abuse, how he felt about me, and several other similar but unimportant tangential questions. The sound of his voice made me nauseous, so I put the phone down, muted myself, and set it to speaker mode so it was not directly in my ear. I had spent years listening to the same tired narratives and excuses that he was now confidently presenting to a court of law as acceptable reasons for unacceptable behavior.

He and his attorney droned on for what felt like hours about everything from how he only stalked the airport so I would "see how much I'd hurt him and take him back" to how he knew it wasn't rape, because "we had a system." I took a sip of my coffee and reached up to rub my neck when my phone buzzed. It was Kathryn with a bit of levity disguised as a serious question: "How is he still going?"

When his attorney finally finished his line of questioning, Kathryn was allowed to cross-examine. She brought his attention to text messages that had been exchanged in the days immediately before the escape. In his previous testimony, he had described himself as a "calm, cool, and collected guy." The text messages in question were paranoid, condescending, and clearly threatening. She had him read the messages out loud and then inquired if that sounded like a "calm, cool, and collected guy" to him.

He huffed, clearly bothered by the implication, and the familiar sound put my nerves back on edge. "I guess not" was all he could muster.

"And can you see how this is threatening?" she continued.

He was flustered but refused to admit it. "If someone who wasn't me said something like that, I can see how it could be interpreted that way," he stammered.

When all the witnesses had been heard and closing arguments had been made, the hearing was given a thirty-minute recess before a decision was to be handed down. I donned my favorite hoodie and walked outside. I tilted my head back, closed my eyes, and let myself feel the sun on my face. This was it. Those on my team and I had done all we could do to convince the courts to see his true colors. Either the order would be upheld and my safety secured, or it wouldn't. It was now in the hands of a judge who, thus far, had maintained his judicial impartiality. A few minutes before the end of recess, I walked back inside and seated myself in an oversized recliner in the living room. The phone rang; we were once again in session. The judge exchanged pleasantries with us and then posed an unexpected question to me: "How do you spell Alfred?"

Confused, I spelled it for him, and he thanked me before going quiet again, except for the sound of a pen on paper. After several more minutes of silence, he began his final comments before handing down his decision. Much of what he said was a blur, comments about having no ill will towards either of us and having heard and considered testimony from both parties—all of the judicial jargon expected in such instances.

The words that made the immense stress and anxiety finally dissipate were these: "I do not find you credible, Mr. Pitfield. I do not find your witnesses credible, and I *do* believe you are a threat to Miss Mackenzie. The order will remain in place, and Alfred the cat is awarded to Miss Mackenzie."

With that, I let out a sharp sigh that I did not know I had been holding, as the relief began to leak from my eyes and trickle down my cheeks. I was unquestionably safe for the first time in months, and the man who had been the cause of so much trauma and fear was being held truly accountable for his actions for the first time in his life.

The judge explained how this ruling affected his rights and asked for confirmation of understanding. "Yes," Andrew hissed, barely able to mask the rage in his voice.

The rest of that day was spent celebrating and reveling in the feeling of legal victory. Little did I realize that now that my physical safety was no longer in question, the real work of healing had to begin.

I had been living with anxiety for as long as I could remember and PTSD for most of my adult life before Andrew had even entered the picture, but the added trauma of those five years sent my mental health into a spiral. Nightmares, panic attacks, dissociation, and sleep paralysis became fixtures in my day-to-day existence, and nothing in my previous symptom management toolkit was working.

After several months of waiting lists, I finally got an appointment with a therapist, whom I still see on a weekly basis almost two years later. I have also been fortunate enough to be partnered with a psychiatric service dog, who has managed to help me in ways that no amount of therapy or medication could.

Healing from trauma is messy, difficult, and sometimes quite painful. There are some days when I don't want to, when I don't feel worthy of the effort and energy it takes to consistently recognize what is me and what is my trauma. Sometimes, the cultivation of radical self-love and self-acceptance that this journey often requires is simply too big of a task. On those days, all I can do is show up for myself and that's okay.

Women are shaped and socialized from our earliest years to believe that our value as people is rooted in how we show up for others in meaningful ways. Mother, sister, friend, partner—all of these roles require us to show compassion, love, and support for other people day in and day out. However, we are hardly, if ever, praised for showing up for ourselves in those same meaningful ways.

I have also learned that to show up for myself is an act of loving kindness towards those closest to me. When I allow the unhealed parts of myself to remain unrecognized and unchecked, that pain eventually seeps into my relationships with others. Although I am not responsible for what happened to me, I am responsible for what happens now. I cannot change the past, but I can continue to show up every day for myself and others. That is where the real power is.

Life now is a world away from what it was when this began. Fear, stress, isolation, and pain have been replaced by joy, stability, support, and connection. Leaving was easily one of the scariest and most difficult things I've ever done. What got me through that experience was the support of the people who cared enough to show up for me, without hesitation or complaint, when I felt most alone in the world. There's a quote I've found myself thinking about often over the last two years:

> "You can pretend to care, but you can't pretend to show up."

ABOUT THE AUTHOR

KATERINA MACKENZIE

Katerina Mackenzie grew up in Northcentral Florida and currently resides in the Pacific Northwest with a small menagerie, including Kai the curmudgeonly Corgi mix, Alfred the Florida swamp cat, and Trek the psychiatric service dog. A graduate of Portland State University with a bachelor's degree in Social Science, she is currently pursuing her master's degree in clinical mental health counseling with the ultimate goal of helping others to escape, survive, and heal from abusive relationships.

9

MY LIFE IS MINE TO WRITE

by Esmirna Caraballo

It's 7:30 p.m., and I can hear the screeching of the timing belt of his white Ford Escort. As I run to the window to make sure it's him, I start to feel excitement stir, but there is a feeling of fear. I didn't know that fear was a warning. I didn't understand how a man I trusted would betray me.

My life is made up of little moments that shaped the stories of trauma and pain, but these moments, in all their horror, created my strength. I have fought to both break free from and embrace my culture. I have survived abuses no child should have ever experienced, but I am not solely my past. My future holds what I lay before it in the present.

In an instant of terror, I flew through the air, stopped abruptly by the hard concrete and a rough hand covering my mouth. The fear, the sweat, and the tears find ways to haunt me, but I am more than this memory, because I write my future.

ಬ•ಛ

I'm a proud, Hispanic woman whose home-life would be considered rough, but in our culture, we don't talk about the negative things happening in the home. It was difficult for me to consider sharing this story, because it meant I was taking another step outside of the cultural box I grew up in.

My childhood in Cleveland, Ohio brought its own big city challenges, but they were only part of what made my young life a difficult one. The motto in our home was, "Do not ask anyone for anything. Earn it yourself, or you will look bad." In short, this meant take any job you can get, earn a degree, and find a good paying career that will support you. Building a business of your own was not even on the table of dreams.

For all practical purposes, I was an only child. There were periods in my life where siblings played a role, but they were brief and their absence painful. By the time I was nine years old, I could cook and keep up the household as any "good wife" could do. To me, it was normal. Many girls my age that I knew were doing the same thing.

As a teenager, however, my responsibilities grew, and the rest of the family's responsibilities shrank. It was the platform I think I needed to prepare me for adulthood, but as a child, I felt used and alone. When I was fourteen years old, my mother experienced an accident that caused her to lose her mobility for almost a year. My tasks became harder, and not having anyone to help us was difficult. I sacrificed my time at school to take care of her. Some family would come by, but one family member caused a feeling of both excitement and fear.

༺•༻

He was thirty-one years old. I knew he was coming by the high-pitched sound of his car. The sound still haunts me to this day. He was related to my stepfather, but he would come to visit nearly every day at 7:30 p.m., like clockwork.

At first, I was happy to have family around. I had been so lonely and doing so much on my own. I welcomed the help. In time, I started to feel something for him. It was a young girl's infatuation, at first. He was older, friendly, and nice to me.

He kept coming. I'd hear his car and run to the window. Excitement would wash over me. Then, one day, I noticed a weird feeling taking the place of my excitement. It was fear, and I couldn't explain it. In the beginning, his normal routine was to greet us, join us for a meal, and enjoy a cup of coffee—a Hispanic tradition. But his behavior began to change, and he started to use the bathroom at least three times every visit. I found it strange, and if I used the bathroom directly after him, I would notice unusual hairs in the sink. They turned out to be pubic hairs. Not truly knowing what they were at that age, I would clean it off and go on with my business.

One day, he came over, and I was by myself in the kitchen. My step-dad was not around, and my mom was sleeping in her room. He shoved me against the wall and began kissing me forcefully. I tried to get away, but he was too strong. I kept battling and struggling with him until he pushed me down the stairs to our basement. The concrete connected with my back, but I ignored the pain and got up. I was so scared and unsure of what was going to happen next. I started to run up the stairs, but he started down them and knocked me back to the bottom again. That was when he started to molest me. His hand covered my mouth to smother my screams. I don't know how, but I finally wiggled out from underneath him. By then, it was too late. The damage had been done, despite getting away before he could finish.

I ran up the stairs, crying, and locked myself in the bathroom. My tears didn't stop. He finally left. I pulled myself back together, left the bathroom, and went out to the kitchen. I continued with the chores I had been working on when he showed up and never said anything about it.

He came back that evening at his usual time. The timing belt howled, but this time I did not go to the window. I hid in my room and hoped my step-dad would not call me to make the coffee. Of course, he did, and I had to face my rapist.

I was terrified. I avoided looking at the man who had ruined my innocence, but I could feel his eyes staring at me. I made the coffee and served everyone as normal. This time, though, I stayed with my mom in her room. He continued to come by, and I would try to stay as far away from him as I could, but any chance he got, he would try to steal a kiss from me or touch me inappropriately.

Eventually, a woman, who understood brujeria (witchcraft), alerted my step-dad to what this man was doing to me. My rapist was doing what we call "a working" on me. As we followed the directions from the woman, we discovered the man had stolen a pair of my white underwear, written on them, and placed his pubic hairs all over them. We followed the woman's instructions to get rid of the panties. That was when my step-dad realized what his relative had been doing to me.

The very same night, at 7:30 p.m., the screeching of his timing belt sounded down the street. As the man attempted to enter the house, my step-dad threw him out and told him to never return. We later learned that he had been accused of sexually assaulting a five- and six-year-old. That's when he finally went to jail.

I was seventeen years old when the phone rang, and I heard his voice on the other end of the line. Emotions flooded my body. I quickly hung up. I was filled with a sense of relief when I was told he would serve twenty-five years in prison, but I felt the relief would only be temporary. I feared the day he would be released.

ಙ•ಬ

So many things happened to me as a child that should never have happened, but I fell into the cultural belief that you do not mention the negative things. I didn't blame anyone, but I couldn't wait to escape into adulthood. When I hit twenty years old, I left my home and never looked back.

I married and became pregnant that year. I found myself doing things I should've done in my teen years—going out with friends, shopping like every girl does, and coming home as late as I could. I quickly realized I couldn't continue making up for my teen years, because I was already married and about to be a mother.

Being a wife was not so hard. I had already experienced a lot of what a good wife does as child. However, becoming a mom created a lot of fear and anxiety for me. I had not been around little children and didn't know what to expect. In my culture, the parents usually don't fully prepare us for this part of our lives. I definitely did not want to fail as a mom, and my age felt like a challenge, too.

I began to question why God would give me a baby girl at my age. I was too young to be a mom. Then, the fear consumed me that she would encounter a man like I did and experience the same type of trauma. I didn't think having a girl was ideal, but ready or not, I was a mom. I needed to find a way to put the past behind me and be the best mom I could be. As we both continue to grow older, I have come to realize she is the sister and best friend I needed in my life. She has taught me so many lessons, and I can't imagine life without her.

Having my daughter in my life gave me the strength to go to college, so I could create a career. I wanted to show her what a strong woman could do, if she tried hard enough. Years later, I had a son, and as I continued to raise my children, I graduated from college. I knew I wanted to erase the past by making positive changes in my life. I did not want my children to experience the kind of things I had been through in my youth.

I married my husband at such a young age, and I've learned so much in this marriage. I have changed, since those early days, and continue to change. Our life is not always easy, but neither is it too hard. We share in both good times and bad. Our hearts are full and have also been broken. I learned that marriage is not always "us against the world," but that it can be two people fighting for what they feel is right.

ಬ•ಐ

Throughout my life, I have learned that some people are there only for a season, to teach us a single lesson, while others are there to stand with us through thick and thin. Though the pain of deceit and losing a friend is real, I'm thankful for the season with them, because I was able to grow and gain a better understanding of myself and people in general.

I took my education and all of my life's lessons and built a career. I built a minority- and female-owned business, fighting my way up while having kids, being married, and learning to break cultural habits. It hasn't always been easy, and there are challenges almost every day. I am very proud of my accomplishments.

My business began in Ohio in 2011, where there were few resources and more than enough challenges. My world almost came crashing down when I lost my office, clients, and eventually myself. It was also during this time I experienced another personal pain that caused me to make many mistakes with people I met, walk away from my marriage, walk away from business, and even step away from the day-to-day lives of my children. To make matters worse, my rapist was released from prison, and the sound of the screeching car began to haunt my dreams.

I felt lost in the challenges I was facing, and I was facing them alone. I fell further and further into the darkness, until in 2016, I made the decision to leave Ohio behind and move my family and my business to Florida. It was a fresh start for all of us.

It took nearly two years to settle into our new lives, but I finally relaunched my business in January 2018. The city I live in is small in comparison to where I grew up. It was difficult for me to navigate at first, because I was not only a new citizen but also a minority. But in 2019, I found an amazing support system with a group of professionals who helped and guided me to the right path, and my business began to flourish and grow. I also found the willpower to co-create the Hispanic Business Council, and it has become a home not only for the Hispanic community, but the entire minority and small business communities.

☙ • ❧

I ran into my rapist on a visit to Cleveland a couple years ago. Anger filled me, as the memories came flooding back. I wanted to hurt him the way he had hurt me and other children, but I stepped away and made sure I would not run into him on the visit again. In 2021, we received word that he had fallen ill and was in the hospital. I finally got some closure when I heard he passed away later that year, with no one to keep him company.

Today, as I continue to grow my business, raise my kids, and finally find myself, I know I have been given the opportunity to be a community leader—to reach out to those who are in need and listen to those who need someone to hear them out. It is fulfilling to help those who want to grow in different ways from personal to business.

I can easily thank those persons who have come into my life and have helped me see the person I am and can be. It does not require an army of people, but that one person who will help me find the strength to tell my story and be my authentic self. Because of this, I find it easier to live better, and I understand that change does not need to be scary. In fact, it can be good.

I know karma will play out for all those who wronged me in my youth. We go through chapters in our lives, and some occur on a daily basis. I still have struggles, but that is normal. After all, the cultural mindset of how I was raised stays with me, but it doesn't need to control me. Even through the hardships, I have come to realize that I can change my circumstances by finding myself. I continue to grow and learn more about myself every day. The changes I make may be subtle, but they may also startle myself and other people with how drastic they will be. That's the thing about growth. It can be small or it can be large. It happens when it's meant to happen.

We all have goals. We may not complete them all, but I know that even if I do not meet the goals I have set, I can still love myself. The ebb and flow of life can be challenging, but I will no longer allow it to stop me. It will no longer change my perspective of the life I want to live. It is never too late to accept who you are, and I accept and love myself for who I am today and who I will become. I am the author of my life.

ABOUT THE AUTHOR

ESMIRNA CARABALLO

Esmirna Caraballo is a Hispanic woman and owner of Esmirna's Notary, Accounting & Tax Services, along with two more small businesses in medical records and collections. Esmirna has earned medical degrees and has an accounting degree. She is a board member and Executive Chair of Finance for the Better Business Bureau, co-founder of the Hispanic Business Council of Ocala, and winner of the Best of the Best Ocala Business Award for her accounting firm two years in a row (beginning in 2020).

10

SHATTERED BUT NOT BROKEN

by Dana (Olmstead) Krull

There was a pattern in my life: experiences that bridged me from one to the next. The first one I remember was at nine, when I accompanied my mom to a weight-loss meeting. She wanted company—the group wanted to include me—but it was the first time I felt imperfect. The scale judged me, and the women handed me a book to track the mocking numbers.

My confidence diminished, and the pattern was reinforced in my early teens. One boy taught me my value with his lies, and another showed me my value when he ignored the word "no." By the time I was in my twenties, most of my relationships were unhealthy. I felt undervalued and imperfect. Without the love and support of a few, true friends, I would not have known how a healthy relationship could look, but it wasn't enough. I still felt unworthy.

That's when I met him—the love of my life—or so I thought. He was fun, made me feel special. His smile lit me up, and I felt like I was seeing the world in an entirely new light. We had lots of adventures, many good memories, lots of laughter. I experienced things I never even had on my radar. I discovered how much I loved the outdoors: camping, hiking, boating, and hunting. I realized I missed the fishing I did as a child. I love to travel. I love to try new things. I am much more adventurous than I ever thought I was.

We traveled domestically and internationally. We spent three weeks in Europe! We went to Germany, Austria, Liechtenstein, Switzerland, Italy, and England. And after eight years of being together, we became engaged on that trip. It felt like a fairytale. I had never dreamt I'd make it to Italy, the country my Dad's mother immigrated from. We picked out my ring in Florence on Ponte Vecchio, and jumped on a train to Rome; he asked me to be his wife in front of the Trevi Fountain.

A year later, we were married in the presence of immediate family and close friends in front of the Grand Tetons in Wyoming. It was beautiful and memorable. The lodge later sent us a certificate for the most romantic wedding of the year. We had a wonderful honeymoon camping through Wyoming, Montana, North Dakota, and Northern Minnesota, before returning home. Everything seemed to be falling into place. We had a nice home, loving family, and wonderful friends, and now, we were husband and wife.

Our one-year anniversary was approaching when I discovered that old habits die hard. There was another woman in his life. But just like several times before we were married, the right words were spoken. He promised me he would stop with other women. I believed it. I bought it—hook, line, and sinker. I'm not sure if it was the fact that we were married that sparked something, but I did feel something new in my reaction. This was different from the times before we were married. We had made vows in the presence of family and friends. We had committed to each other in a way we weren't committed to anyone else.

My heart was broken. I wasn't just angry and hurt this time. I didn't just feel unworthy or not enough. I felt betrayed and crushed. I started to realize I couldn't control how he reacted to me, but I could control how I reacted to him. I started to focus on myself more. I focused on being healthy and doing things that made me happy.

A few months after discovering what my husband had been doing behind my back, I found yoga. I've always enjoyed exercising, but yoga was one of the things I hadn't tried, yet. It started to become a part of my regular routine. I still remember my first class. Something really resonated with me, and I knew I needed more yoga in my life. That studio would become a place I went to heal. I met some amazing people. They helped me see the strength I had inside and challenged me. I was pushed physically, mentally, and emotionally. They encouraged me to make myself a priority, because I wasn't sure how to do that. I started to nurture myself inside and out.

Yoga made me feel like I was fine-tuning things I was already doing or knew about. It wasn't just about the poses I did on my mat. It was so much more. It was about connecting my mind, body, and soul. It was the first time I realized that the mind would give up long before the body. If you can gain mental strength, you'll be surprised at how much more you can do physically. And I found I could do more emotionally, too. My mind was my strongest muscle, and I had been neglecting it. I wasn't nurturing it or giving it the respect that it needed. Yoga was one of the ways I not only learned to love and accept myself more, but also a way I learned to gain strength. The studio was a safe place I went to take a pause from the world outside and focus on healing myself.

In 2010, my husband and I decided that we were ready to have children and later that year, I became pregnant. From the beginning it felt too good to be true. I was nervous with no real explanation as to why. My mom's birthday is mid-

January, and we decided we would tell everyone then. Everyone was really excited for us. A new chapter.

In early February, I had a nightmare that I still vividly remember. I think that was the night our baby died. At our next ultrasound, they couldn't find a heartbeat. They sent us to the hospital for another ultrasound. Still no heartbeat. Our little baby was inside of me, lifeless. Gone, but still there. My heart broke in a way I couldn't have ever imagined. I cried like I had never cried before.

I felt lost and in some type of weird limbo. I was pregnant, but I wasn't. Our sweet baby would never be held. We would never see their face. It was about three weeks later when my doctor said we couldn't wait any longer for my body to release the baby. I was scheduled to have the baby removed a week before my birthday. I felt empty and lost. My husband didn't know what to do. He was lost, but in a different way.

In July, I would have another miscarriage, but I kept it quiet and told only a few people. I was heartbroken and ashamed. I felt like I was the one killing the babies.

In early September, I started to feel hope return, and we decided to try one more time. This pregnancy was to be successful, but not easy. I was very tired the entire time and had little support on the homefront. People commented that my husband acted more like a single man than a husband about to become a father. He spent a lot of time away from the house and away from me.

Childbirth wasn't any easier than my pregnancy. After almost eight hours in labor at the hospital, our son was delivered via emergency C-section. It was scary. The first two months after his birth were hard. Our son was wonderful, but I didn't feel supported. Recovering from a C-section wasn't easy, and breastfeeding wasn't going well for our son and me. I felt distant from my husband, but I thought that was due to becoming parents while still trying to maintain and maneuver the life we had before our son was born. My husband was gone a lot—the usual working and with friends.

Our son was nine months old when I discovered my husband had been cheating again. I kicked him out, but after a few hours, I let him back in. I assured him that I was done with his cheating. I would give him one more chance, but if it ever happened again, our son and I would be gone. He promised me, again, that there would be no more "other women." I wanted to believe him, but how could I?

For our next wedding anniversary, he took me back to where we were married. Just the two of us. It was a fun trip. On our anniversary, we renewed our marriage vows with the judge, who had originally married us. We enjoyed dinner at the lodge where we were first married. We hiked some trails we hadn't seen before and explored a few other things in and around town that were new to us.

It didn't take long after our trip for things to go back to how they were. I felt distant from my husband again. I couldn't figure out how we could be sitting in the same room, yet feel like there was a valley between us. Time passed, and I think I just accepted our routines. I wanted us to be a family, but it really didn't feel like we were. Sure, in pictures we looked great. When people saw the three of us, they saw a family.

Over the next few years, we'd buy and renovate a house. Our son would celebrate two birthdays in that house, before I truly felt the marriage was over. I finally knew, or maybe I accepted, that something was broken and would never be fixed. I saw the patterns that had been repeating over and over. I saw how things progressively got worse—how our relationship declined over the years. I thought I had failed. Really, we had failed each other.

For us, for our son, for me, I had to give it one last attempt. I proposed marriage counseling as my last olive branch. He wasn't happy, but he accepted. Right after our first session, I discovered he was cheating again. I couldn't understand him, and I was done trying. What the hell! He always made me feel like a nag or nosy for asking him how his day was. He made me feel crazy and stupid. Maybe I was, I thought.

One day, I decided that being alone would be better than being with him. Being alone meant that I wouldn't have to wonder where he was, who he was with, or who that was on his phone or the computer. I wouldn't have to wonder if he'd be home for dinner and to put our son in a bath, read him a book at bedtime, or tuck him in for the night. I wouldn't have to wonder if someone would help me bring in the groceries, clean the house, do the laundry, or anything else. Alone meant all I had to worry about was our son and myself.

A few months after our first marriage counseling session, I told him I wanted a divorce. He wouldn't sign the papers. I'm pretty sure he thought I'd change my mind. A few months later, I was contacted by a stranger who would validate every suspicion I had over the last few years. It was worse than I had thought. It was one of those moments where you can't believe something like this happened to you. I was rattled to my core. I felt like I had no idea who I married. How could someone who claimed to love me and our son so much do the things he had done?

Things at home got worse before they got better. We finally separated and sold our house. The month we sold our house, the closing on my new home was postponed two or three times. During that time I was also laid off from my job of eleven years. I would be laid off for a year and a half before I would find a new job. It was a hard time for me, but a very healing time. I took time to concentrate on my son and me. During his first year of school, I was available to volunteer, and I could easily make his events and programs.

I said yes to a spiritual pilgrimage to Peru. I traveled with eight others from the United States and a Peruvian travel guide, and we were accompanied on several days by Q'ero shamans. It was a time of reflection, release, and rebirth. I spent the first two days feeling like I was in a deep detox. I was so excited to be in Peru with these amazing people, but inside, I was finally letting go of things that needed to be released—feelings and emotions I had put on hold. I felt very grounded in Peru and closer to myself again. I started to remember who I was before I felt like I had shattered into a million pieces.

I followed up the trip to Peru with a two hundred-hour yoga teacher training. Then, two more yoga teacher training sessions. I put my training to good use when

I found a volunteer opportunity at a local shelter for women and children of abuse. My volunteering helped me just as much as it helped the women I had the honor to guide through a yoga session. Those women wanted to feel safe, to be seen, to be heard, to have hope, and to heal. I gave them the space for all of that, along with some self-care they could take with them. The sessions ranged from silly, when the kids would join us, to a place of peace.

My son and I rescued a dog and became his forever home. The day I accepted the offer for my new job, I also received notification that my divorce was final. I didn't know if I should cheer, cry, or take a nap! It was a very emotional day. It felt like a new chapter was about to begin.

Through everything, there were some days where the only thing that got me through the day was my son. He was my reminder, my light. I want to be a good role model for him. I want him to be proud of where he comes from. I knew I had to lead by example for him to be strong and to be a good person. He had a front row seat, and he was watching every move, every word, every action. I want him to always feel safe, loved, and enough. I want him to have all the tools he needs to become the wonderful man I know he will be. That means that I let him see me ask for help, I let him see me cry, and I let him see that I'm still learning.

We live in a home where our family rules hang on the wall: Share. Be kind. Smile. Laugh and have fun. Keep your promises. Say I'm sorry. Forgive. Do your best. Say please and thank you. Respect one another. Always tell the truth. Be silly. Be patient. Hug often. And, most importantly, love one another. We do all of those things together.

I've been told it was a beautiful thing to watch, the way I handled everything. I remember hearing stories of the butterfly coming out of its cocoon. The way the phoenix rises from the ashes. A mosaic created from the pieces that had been broken. More beautiful than before. There were a lot of tears when I was alone.

When I look back on those years, I can now see and appreciate the change and growth that happened. I proved that I'm not the kind of woman who sits in a corner and gives up. I knew a better life was waiting, but I had to want it enough to fight for it. I have been blessed to find a beautiful soul who loves my son and our crazy fur baby as much as he loves me. There is still more healing to do and old habits I need to break. But I have learned it is okay to accept help, and I don't always have to face everything alone. I try to never say anything to myself that I wouldn't say to someone I love.

I still have days where just making it through the day is enough.

I need to remember that my value is not defined by a number in a book, how a high school boyfriend treated me, by relationships that turned toxic, or the dark thoughts about myself I've let make a home in my head. I know I am loved and appreciated by the people who matter. I have learned it is not only okay to love yourself, but also necessary. The way you love yourself shows others how you need to be loved. If only we could all see ourselves through the eyes of those who truly love us. We could see how *amazing* we are!

ABOUT THE AUTHOR

DANA (OLMSTEAD) KRULL

Dana Olmstead is a daughter, mother, wife, friend, yoga instructor, lover of nature, and, by day, a professional for twenty-four-plus years in the financial industry. Filling her cup consists of time with her son, family, friends, and in nature. Dana is a yoga teacher, and the training brought her to a volunteer opportunity where she not only shares her passion for yoga, but also her gift of compassion and letting others know they are not alone. She currently lives in the Midwest with her son and their dog.

11

IN CASE OF EMERGENCY, BREAK GLASS

by Shereese Floyd

I opened the bedroom door where he kept his clothes—his black duffel bag, gone. His folded clothes on the laundry table, gone. I opened the door to our bedroom, dropped to my knees and looked under the bed. His beloved watch collection, gone. My knees buckled as I tried to stand. "Maybe, he's just gone for a few days," I thought.

He was distant when he came home from spending Christmas with his daughter in Philadelphia. He didn't talk much. Sensing my misgivings, he assured me our relationship was the best it had ever been. But something was off. Something did not feel its normal wrong side of right. I went into my office to retrieve a watch I'd yet to give him. It was a surprise gift, a watch to symbolize a commitment of time and to celebrate the one-year anniversary of our baptism as a couple. It, too, was gone.

I stood in the hallway of our home, replaying every conversation and every action from every room. My body was burning with the truth; my mind needed to hide. He was gone, along with any hope he was simply gone for the night. But this is not the first time my husband had abandoned our relationship nor was it the first incident of stolen time.

Our courtship was a Hallmark card come to life. Every word I'd ever dreamed, he said. Every promise I could ever think, he declared. I was his soulmate, someone whom he prayed for, a woman unlike anyone he'd ever met. We thought the same thoughts. We finished each other's sentences.

I didn't fall in love. I dove, heart first, into my fantasy—filled with the constant adulation and praise of a lover's lexicon meant only for me. He was a self-proclaimed knight who showed up to slay anyone who got near me, and he did. He fiercely protected me. I felt kinder and gentler. Friends and family noted my perkier self. I had found my person. We were *#relationshipgoals*.

I sat in the living room watching my then fiancé standing at the sink washing dishes. We were conversing about the day. Our conversation was tense, as we talked about his ex with whom he'd spent the night. I said one word too many in a tone he didn't like, and he tested the waters.

I heard a high-pitch whistle and felt a breeze on my ear before hearing a loud crash and being pelted by what felt like prickly rain. He had thrown a glass from across the room. It had landed just inches from my head. Chards of glass had pinged off the window sill behind me, landing in various places around my face and neck. I looked up and saw the hand that had held the glass moments ago was now empty and my shirt full of the pieces of a shattered illusion.

Fuck, I thought. Another one of these relationships. The same man, different face, but this was more intrusive and direct. I was shocked at the boldness of the action.

I remember the look on his face. His breathing labored. Unsure. He had just revealed himself, and the uncertainty of my reaction loomed over us. Time and space slowed down as we moved through the quicksand of brokenness.

I got up off the sofa, sumo wrestler style, shaking off the pieces of glass. My eyes and face had been spared, but there was a twinge over my right shoulder. I reached back and felt a small tear in my t-shirt. I'd been cut.

I grabbed my keys and left the house, only to retreat to my car for a few minutes. Remembering this was my place, I went back, hoping to find him packing his things, but he wasn't. He was standing in the exact spot at the sink, as if stuck in time.

His face was different. Less oh shit, more damn. His blinks, the morse code of manipulation.

I didn't say a word. I didn't tend to my wound. I went to lie down. I felt the blood trickling down my back. After a few moments, he came in, lay down on the bed, spooned me, scooped me up in his arms, performing acts one and two of the apology tour and following chapter and verse of the abuser's playbook.

"I'm sorry," he said.

The words I wanted to say got stuck in my throat. I wanted to tell him to leave. I wanted him to go away and never come back, but something about him felt worth it. I was already making excuses for his behavior. Choking back tears and what was left of my dignity, I responded, "Okay," pulling him closer.

This is when I revealed myself to him. This is when he knew I had no boundaries.

Several months later, in a ceremony performed by the State of Pennsylvania, the bride wore white, the groom wore shackles, and sheriff's deputies served as witnesses in a ceremony one could only describe as theater. I married an alleged murderer before he became a convicted one. He was awaiting accountability for a crime he'd committed years ago under his given name, a name I learned upon his dramatic capture, when a team of US Marshalls descended on us in a scene to rival a Lifetime movie production.

Two years after taking his name, I stood in another Pennsylvania courtroom behind him, rather than beside him, and watched as my life changed instantly and forever when he was sentenced to 12.5 to twenty-five years. With the finality of the gavel, I knew everything in my life would be different and difficult.

Grieving a person who is still alive is very real. Despite any reservations I had, the heartstrings grew tighter. There was never a question of whether or not I would keep my commitment to him; I'd made that choice with the promise of "until death do us part." For better or worse, I was now Mrs. GE-6309. The cycle of abuse had already begun and didn't stop during the incarceration.

I noticed pretty early on there was no space for me in the relationship. Any mention of how hard life was for me as a single-married woman was met with a turning table of focusing on the real pain—his life inside on the island of misfit boys. Mine was a life of diminishing returns. Each year, I got smaller in relevance, while my scorecard got bigger. My imperfections as a prisoner's wife were tallied and recorded for posterity.

Within those twelve years, I grew up and realized this was not a life I wanted. It was a burden, more than a celebration of love. It was the revelation I needed to leave. I sent divorce papers right after he made parole. He signed. It was done. But it wasn't the final chapter.

A mere eight months after his release, the ink barely dry on version one of this tragedy, I remarried him on Valentine's Day. Together again, under the same roof with all the same issues. Over the years, the abuse escalated. It started with name calling and criticism, grabbing, pushing, throwing things, and smashing in walls with his hands or my body. All of which I thought I could handle. We were going to beat the odds. I was his ride or die chick to whom he had sworn nothing would come between us—ever. If only I did more or made more money to relieve his stress, the abuse would stop.

I was tethered to darkness—playing macabre games of false communication. I was on a merry-go-round of toxicity, and I was turning into him. He was the person who promised to protect me, but in the end, the protection I needed was from him.

☼•☼

I don't remember what we were arguing about. It was the middle of the night. I was in bed, and he was upset about something I said or did previously in the evening.

He lived on the edge of explosiveness, quickly antagonistic and defensive. Although he had a playful nickname for his condition—Grumpelstiltskin—his anger was no laughing matter. I danced on eggshells— a constant arabesque en pointe—careful not to set him off and constantly asking if he were okay. He would say, "Anger is not my only emotion." True, but it was the prevailing one and the one

I encountered most often. On this night, there was no dancing. I stood flat-footed in the ensemble of events.

He paced back and forth between the living room and the bedroom, drawing closer to the bed each time he appeared. I got up to get dressed. I was cloaked in layers of vulnerability, in an enclosed space, without clothing, and each time he entered the room, the entry (and exit) was blocked. I needed to minimize my risk. Shirt and shoes required.

Once dressed, I timed my movements to match his, so I could get into the living room where I had more space. I tuned out most of his rantings, but his inquiries and commands rang through loud and clear. "Where are you going? Sit your ass down!" he yelled. I complied, taking a seat on the couch next to my bag and keys.

I had learned to decipher the levels of his rage. Tonight, he came in hot. Calming him down was a skill I had not mastered, partially because he didn't like being told what to do, and my intervening only made it worse. My usual course of action was to disengage and let him rant until he got tired. His rants could go for hours, but even five minutes of him raging in a high pitch seemed like an eternity.

I had to be strategic about my next move. He was hip to my survival techniques. Disengaging and/or getting into a safe position was not always the right approach.

A couple months prior, he had pulled out a duffle bag from his car. It contained women's clothing that didn't belong to me. He tried to convince me the pieces were mine, and when that didn't work, he followed up by trying to convince me he was doing a favor for someone.

I couldn't be angry, because he'd overtaken my right to be. The onus flipped. I found myself defending my position, as he was now the wounded party. How dare I impugn his character? I couldn't listen anymore. He raged. I disengaged. He ranted. I moved. He got louder. I kept moving until he grabbed me by my throat and pushed me up against a wall. My eyes widened; my spine stiffened.

Up until this point, the abuse had a vocabulary I knew how to speak, but this was a language I didn't understand. I vacillated between staying still and fighting back. He was freakishly strong, and he had a good grip on my neck. I noted the look on his face, his eyes black with entitlement. He commented at my surprise, "Yeah," signaling his ownership and lack of remorse. This was a man who held two positions in our marriage: "I will stop your heart" or "You are the safest woman in America." With his fingers gripping my airway, I believed the former, and thus, I stayed still until he released me.

This night, I sat on the couch waiting for my moment and praying for the best. When he stopped pacing and paused for a bathroom break, I saw an opening. I grabbed my bag and keys, unlocked and opened the front door, and unlocked and opened the screen door, hastening down the stairs onto the sidewalk, the flashing headlights letting me know the car was open and ready for my escape.

I knew he was behind me as the screen door flung open and smashed into the wall. No sooner had I gotten into the car and hit the lock than I felt the car jerk. I looked at him. He was holding the door handle to my car. I turned back to put the key in the ignition to start the car when I heard the clink of glass. He kicked in the window with steel toe boots. He kept kicking the car. I was stunned watching a man all of fifty years old have a tantrum to put a five-year-old to shame. I was trapped in my own two positions of needing to ensure my safety versus wanting to console him. The car rocked back and forth with each hit. Finally, I drove off in a fog, feeling outside of my reality.

It was 2:00 a.m. I had nowhere to go. I didn't know what I was going to do. I ended up in a Walmart parking lot, taking pictures of the external damage, while trying to access and soothe the internal ones.

I sat in the parking lot for hours, living out the consequences of my decisions: to stay knowing he was violent and abusive, to cover up and perpetuate the lies, to portray him as a savior, to act as his communication manager and PR rep, to put his mental needs above my own. This was the convergence of my choices.

The truth was I had places to go, but I would have to explain the man I had versus the man I had created. I wasn't yet ready to do that, so I went home.

I waited for the cooling-off period—giving him time to put the monster to rest. When I got back to the house, he said, "I'm not going to hurt you." I went inside and went to bed, eyes wide open—shirt and shoes required. He had already hurt me, and he could (and would) hurt me, again.

Later, when we talked about the incident, I asked, "What would you have done if you had gotten to me?"

"I don't know."

☙•❧

When I stood in that empty hallway realizing he'd left, I couldn't catch my breath. Every rise and fall of my chest felt like a hollowed drum. I suffocated in my agony. Every cell in my body filled with ache and longing. But I wasn't longing for him per se; I longed for what was familiar. I longed for a fix. But this time, the fix I needed was not coming.

The little girl in me performing for love had to put down her beggar's cup and simply stand in an uncomfortable truth that I didn't know how to exist without auditioning for affection and the right to simply be. I longed for the space between awareness and awakening. It was easier to pretend I didn't know I deserved better.

I am not responsible for the abuse, but I am responsible for healing, and the way I talked about healing was all wrong. In the beginning, I asked:
- "Why did he do this to me?"
- "Why did he hurt me like this?"
- "Why didn't he respect me?"

Those were the wrong questions. The better questions were:
- "Why did I stay so long?"
- "Why were my standards so low?"
- "Why didn't I respect and protect myself?"
- "What did this pain come to teach me?"

I was not processing a breakup or end of a marriage. I was processing forty-nine years of unhealings. This was the making of a new me, and in this tale, no one was coming to save me, protect me, or shield me. My *perception* of self became my *reflection* of self.

Amidst the wreckage of my being, I pick through the rubble of shattered selfies—self-esteem, self-awareness, self-respect, self-confidence, self-worth. I exist as shards of a person I don't know or recognize. I hold on to the one selfie left unscathed—the one not damaged in the fall—self-doubt. I clean it up and tuck it firmly into the pocket of my spirit.

Nothing and no one is going to break me again, not with this by my side.

The problem with holding on to self-doubt is that it's the onramp to a highway paved with self-loathing, insecurity, and uncertainty—the road to victimhood.

As I sift through my remains, I prick myself on pieces of light, pieces of love, pieces of hope, pieces of laughter. I see glimpses of the woman I was, but moreover, the woman I desire to be.

And as I sit with myself and outside of myself, cursing and admiring all that I am, if there is any hope of being different, I need to see these shattered pieces as the makings of the mosaic to become more.

In fact, I am *not* broken at all. I *don't* need to be fixed.
- I am wounded. Wounds need *time* to scar over.
- Broken is just that. Wounds are a *foundation*.
- Broken is just that. Wounds *heal*.
- Broken is just that.

As I work at this new composition of me, I install new data, an alert—selfies do not work in the hands of anyone outside of myself, and a tripwire of self-trust, whereby if I choose to bypass my intuition, I am solely responsible for the damage caused by my internal landmine.

I was wounded. But, I am regenerating.

The best and most healing balm available is self-love. For it is the only selfie that breathes life, eradicates self-doubt, and reminds me: In case of emergency, break glass.

ABOUT THE AUTHOR

SHEREESE FLOYD

Shereese Floyd, owner of Witness My Life, is a storytelling strategist who helps women raise their voices and tell their stories so that they are impossible to ignore. Shereese is the author of *Become the Greatest Story Ever Told: Making a Memoir*. She received a Cicero Speechwriting award for her TEDx Talk "The Secret to Healing the World." She believes sharing our stories is the one way to bring the world together.

12

FROM VICTIMHOOD TO WARRIORHOOD

by Connie Rose

November 2, 2008, my fifty-second birthday. I'm free, finally free! No more looking over my shoulder or in dark shadows of the night, worrying he will come after me, my daughter, young girls, or their mothers. I can finally breathe—a long, visible breath for the world to see. This is the day my father—the first of many abusers, my trafficker, my pimp—died.

I thought my day of freedom was going to be nine months earlier. My fifty-three-year-old brother Steve called, and in a frantic, childlike voice said, "Dad is dying. Did you hear me? Dad is dying! Sissy, I need you to come to the hospital. I can't do this without you!" The Greek priest was on his way to give our dad his last rights. The last thing I wanted to do was drive forty-five minutes to the hospital, after having an injection in my back, to see the man who had taken away my childhood.

I immediately called my best friend Linda, who was more like a sister, shrieking as I apprised her of the situation, begging her to guide me, to tell me what to do. All the while my inner child, little Connie, was stomping her feet and saying, "I won't go! I won't go! Let him die!"

Linda gently, yet firmly, reminded me of a speech on forgiveness I had given the week before. The audience was comprised mostly of women who had endured one form or another of abuse. A thin, silver-haired woman, whom I guessed to be in her early eighties, shared with everyone, for the first time, that she too was a survivor of incest. Then I heard, "How will you react when you hear your father has died?" It took every ounce of verbal restraint to not say, "He deserves to die!" My response: Over the course of my adult life, I have forgiven that man several times and for different reasons.

After speaking with Linda, I had my answer. I would take the lead from my brother. He was a grown man trapped inside of his six-year-old mind. I felt responsible for making sure he was okay. Darn co-dependency showed up again! Off I went, driving into the sunset on a road with several twists and turns. The sky blessed me with a beautiful palette of colors, as I reflected on what the heck I was going to do once I arrive at the hospital and his room. The last time I saw my father was November 2000, when his sister had passed away.

I vividly remember asking the nurse on duty if I could see my father Andy's chart. I wanted to make sure it stated he was a "registered sex offender." I couldn't believe my eyes. Nowhere on his chart did it even mention those words. I quickly said to the nurse, "Do you know who this man is and what he has done to women and girls?"

The nurse asked me how I had found the strength to come and see him on his deathbed. All I had to do was look over at my brother and she had her answer. My brother dreamed his entire life our father would be like Ward Clever in *Leave It to Beaver*. We both dreamed of the day we would be free…free from the abuse so many endured, our mother, hundreds of others, and us, his natural-born children.

As the nurse and I were talking, waiting for the Greek priest to arrive, suddenly, my father grunted. Yes, he grunted, calling out my name, "Connie." He hadn't said a word in the past ten days. I remember looking up and thinking to myself, this is a God moment.

My father stayed in the hospital ten more days. Upon his release, he asked me if I would visit him. Once again, I call Linda, "Sis, what do I do now? He wants me to visit him. Have lunch or dinner with him. Help!"

It wasn't easy to see this man. Especially eat a meal with him. I had just finished reading *Tuesdays With Morrie*. I could do something like that: "Tuesdays with Andy." I realized God was giving me a way to finally release the hold my father had on me. The first time we got together, I took out my list of boundaries and explained just how this was going down. I will take you to lunch, dinner, and your doctor's appointments. This is not about you, it's about me and the children and women you sexually abused. We would talk for hours. I needed to know who this man was and why he did the horrible, unmentionable things to me, his own flesh and blood.

At thirteen years old, he was gang raped over a porn magazine an older teen boy showed him. He learned porn and rape were a way to have total power and control over another human being. It took him years to use that power and control. Once he did, he couldn't stop. Even at seventy-nine years old, he was still a pimp.

I am a survivor of over sixteen years of incest, forced pornography, domestic violence, exploitation, and human sex trafficking, all at the hands of a serial sex offender father.

I was sixteen years old, pregnant—ostensibly by an older boyfriend, who knew about the abuse I was enduring daily. He was upset and not sure what he could do. The next words out of his mouth: "We have to get you away from him before you take your own life." My prince, my rescuer, enlisted in the Army. My pregnancy became part of our escape plan: the Army would take care of us. He left for boot camp. We had a plan: after he graduated from boot camp, I would join him, and we would get married. The Army would take care of us.

I remember when it sunk in that I was pregnant. I found myself consumed with this horrible thought: "My father finally had his dream fulfilled; he was having a baby with me." Because I was forced to have sex with my father and so many other men (buyers), I didn't know who the father was. I was scared, alone, and I couldn't follow through with our plans.

With my childhood best friend at my side, I told my parents I was pregnant. My father quickly said, "No worries, your mother and I will raise your baby as if it's our own."

I remember the look on my mother's face and the pit I had in my stomach. We both knew if I had this child, it too would end up being abused. Adoption was not an option; he would fight us for him to keep my baby. My mother, a devout Catholic, who marched on the capitol steps in Tallahassee, Florida with the pro-life movement, found herself searching for a doctor who would perform a late-term abortion.

On August 12th, 1973, my father checked me into Tampa General Hospital to have an intra-amniotic instillation abortion and signed burial documents and paid for a gravesite, to bury my baby girl, whom I named Cindy.

I was checked into a room and told to change into a hospital gown. I was left all alone, lying there on a cold, hard hospital bed, waiting for what was going to happen the next morning—coincidentally, my parents' wedding anniversary. The nurse and doctor came in and injected a solution through the abdomen and into the amniotic sac. All alone in this stark, white hospital room, I delivered my stillborn baby girl. I never got to hold her. All I could do was cry and ask God to forgive me.

From the first inappropriate touch to the last day I lived under his roof, my life consisted of being a commodity: an object to be raped, exploited, bought, and sold. Repeatedly, my father told me, "You are the best of the best. I taught you everything you need to know. All you have to do is use your looks and your body, and you can have anything you want." I grew up believing my worth was in my appearance. When I was lured into prostitution, this belief sunk in deeper. I was nothing but a commodity. The belief carried over into adulthood, my career choices, marriage, and beyond.

My first escape from my father's abuse was getting married at nineteen years old. Back in the Seventies, it wasn't uncommon for young women to get married and not attend college. In 1976, I was engaged to a very nice young man with whom I truly believed I was in love. Reflecting back, I had no concept what love was. Sex was love, and love was sex—a distorted definition I learned from the first person who said he loved me, my father.

My wedding was on a beautiful April day in sunny Florida. My father and I stood at the back of Sacred Heart Catholic Church, waiting for "Here Comes the Bride." My father turned to me and said, "You do not have to go through with this. The limo is waiting, and you and I can escape to another country and live as husband and wife." I have no idea how I made it down the beautiful cathedral aisle to my groom. Unfortunately, our marriage lasted only three-and-a-half years.

In 1982, at twenty-six years old, I married for a second time to a narcissistic, addictive man. He was such a smooth talker, and before I knew it, I had fallen in love with him.

As the years went by, his behaviors escalated to the point I had no choice but to take my two children and leave. I remember the day I made the decision to escape from his clutches. Once again, I sought the wisdom of Linda. A girls' weekend in Orlando. When she took one look at my frail, five-foot-six-inch, one hundred-five-pound body, she knew I was in deep trouble. I was not holding up to the financial and verbal abuse I endured daily from my husband. As we were walking up the stairs at our hotel, I stopped, curled up on the stairs, and began alternating between laughing and crying. My life was slipping away from me. Over and over, I said, "No one protected me as a child. I will do everything in my power to protect my children from this man."

It took me years of therapy and having my two beautiful children to find the strength deep down inside to move past the shame, blame, and guilt I carried around my heart like an anchor for so many years. I was weighed down by feelings of isolation, powerlessness, and entrapment. I had to find a way to bring the light into the darkness—not only for me, but also for the hundreds of my father's victims.

In 1988, just a few short months after my father was arrested and pleaded guilty to engaging in sexual activity with another child and assault against that child, I decided I was more than the crimes committed against me. More than my story. More than a victim. I was a survivor. I was a warrior, ready to break the chains and shine the light on childhood abuse.

The summer of 1992, I walked onto the campus of Barry University, in Miami Shores, Florida. With a pit in my stomach, I walked into the enrollment office and declared "It was my time to finally earn my bachelor's degree in training, development, and adult learning." My husband did everything he could to discourage me. He told me I didn't need a college degree. All I needed was him and to be his arm candy. Before I knew it, graduation was two semesters away. I wasn't ready for my education to end. I walked into the dean's office to inquire about the training, development, and adult learning master's program. The next thing I knew, I was dual enrolled and scheduled to graduate with my master's degree in the spring of 1995. I showed my father and husband! I graduated with honors and spoke at the honors award's ceremony.

It took me over forty years to learn I was not someone's property. I didn't think or believe a man would love me beyond my currency. Real love that doesn't hurt! I am finally in love with a man who cherishes me.

I found that love in my high school sweetheart Rico. Rob, a mutual friend, introduced us when we were teenagers. I was fifteen; Rico was seventeen. He was my knight in shining armor. Nice, sweet, and so handsome. Rico was the first person I ever told about the many forms of abuse I was enduring. On the night I told him, I started crying, and the words just came out of my mouth. He said, "You have to tell your mom what he is doing."

We pulled up to my home in the suburbs of Tampa. Rico turned the engine off and said, "Your dad is not home. I'll wait outside while you go in and tell your mom."

As I was telling her what was happening to me, her Italian temper flared up, and she started screaming—not at me, but at what I was telling her. You see, my mother was also my father's victim. He had raped her when they were dating. Later, she told me all she could see is what he did to her and the abuse she tucked away from her own father. I begged to be sent to a convent or the tobacco fields, where bad girls went in the Sixties and Seventies. She looked around her dream home, with tears in her eyes. "I will tell him to stop. One day you will get married and change your last name. Your brother will carry the family name for the rest of his life."

I realized, in that moment, if I was ever going to get away, I would have to take matters into my own hands.

Our teen dating ended when Rico went off to college. In November 2010, thirty-seven years later, via social media and Rob, we reunited. The love we had for each other was reawakened—a beautiful, unconditional love, where I am valued as a human being, not as a commodity.

I have been truly blessed over the course of the years, despite the abuse I endured. God blessed me with two fantastic children. My son is a men's fashion designer, married to my wonderful daughter-in-love, and I have two incredible grandsons. My daughter is a chiropractor, dating a wonderful man who cherishes her and my grand-dog Rufus. I've had my own radio show, worked for Revlon Cosmetics as a consultant and national trainer, owned a nail salon, taught special education, and was a pharmaceutical dermatology representative.

Since 2010, I have had the honor and privilege to walk alongside survivors of sexual abuse, exploitation, and human sex trafficking. Standing in their resilience, in their personal power, together we give a voice to the voiceless. I am the founder and executive director of an anti-sex trafficking non-profit, sit on the board for another non-profit, and was recently appointed as the Southern Co-president for a provider network in the State of Florida, which serves youth who are victims of human trafficking.

During a twenty-four-hour period in October 2017, the hashtag #MeToo was shared twelve million times on social media. In response to allegations of sexual assault and rape directed at Hollywood producer Harvey Weinstein, an unprecedented virtual assembly emerged on social media which was public, voluntary, and global. It was like flipping on a light switch in a dark room.

While society was becoming more aware of the physical scars of #MeToo, they were not seeing the emotional ones eating away at our senses of self, the hidden damage we carried under our suit of armor. Women, who have experienced sexual trauma, may have trouble maintaining healthy relationships in the future and either become repressed and unwilling to trust future partners or feel as though they somehow "deserved it" and will continued to engage in risky sexual behaviors.

When I was at my lowest, I felt like no one understand how worthless I felt, carrying the burden of my own abuse and those of my father's victims.

Unveiling the mask, getting to the ugly underbelly of who I really was, took years of soul searching. I walked around like I had so much confidence, hiding behind an invisible mask. My mask protected me from me and from feeling my feelings. From letting the outside world see the real me.

Make-up was part of my mask. I never left my house without a full face of make-up, not even to take the garbage out. I felt ugly without my mask, fearful everyone could see my hurt and know my secret, feeling societal pressure to look a certain way—with everything airbrushed, photo-shopped, and filters trimming down and smoothing out the beautiful flaws that make us unique. I looked at women who were naturally pretty, and I was jealous. It took me years to start loving me, the me God created. Embracing her!

This woman is a *warrior*!
She is *unstoppable*!
Gracefully fragile, beautifully standing.
She is love, life, and transformation.
She is *grace*.
She is *brave*.
She will never stop learning or moving forward.
She is *you*.

Today, no matter what is happening in the world, and no matter how stressful a day I may have, I am grateful I found a way to change my mind and change my life.

ABOUT THE AUTHOR

CONNIE ROSE

Connie Rose is the founder of Victims2Survivors-US, the creator of Moving Beyond Me Too, Get Help, Get Out, Post It Note Initiative, and The Collaboratory: Community Conversations to Eliminate Human Trafficking. She survived child sexual abuse, domestic violence, exploitation, and sex trafficking. Connie's life is dedicated to bringing awareness about the atrocities she and so many others have endured. She is a veteran of the TEDx stage: "What Can You Learn From A Rubber Band?" Connect with her at **www.Victims2SurvivorsUS.org**.

13

SALVAGED SOUL

by Fannie Ocasio

I was poisoned at the age of six. On the day I blindly followed Harvey, this grown man I hardly knew, into that cold, empty room in our mostly unfurnished apartment, my immature mind could not imagine what awaited me. My naiveté and focus on the brown paper bag of toys he had promised lulled me, disarming the warning alarms indicated by the sick feeling in my stomach and the tiny hairs standing up on the back of my neck. As Harvey closed the door behind us, his snakelike aura wrapped tightly around me, as it had my mother. Harvey's intoxicating grip over mom's singleness and insecurity dulled her maternal instincts, leaving both of us vulnerable to the pedophilic python she proudly introduced as her boyfriend to all.

Unlike Mother, Grandma had not been so easily fooled. She hated Harvey from the moment she met him. Before even settling in on Grandma's couch that day, he smugly handed her the empty glass he spit in after drinking the water she offered him. Not just any kind of spit. He hocked a deep, guttural, phlegm-filled foulness that screamed of disdain from the depths of his throat. As if that had not been enough, when he met me—the dad-less, love-starved kid that I was—he angrily reacted to my childish antics and demanded, "Take this kid away from me before I knock her upside down." This would cause a rift in Mom and Grandma's alliance, laying wide open the door to opportunity for the predator to prey.

After my mom and dad divorced, Dad's disinterest in fatherhood would leave a gaping hole in my childhood foundation, crippling my development. Harvey, however forced, was the new man in our lives, and for Mother's sake, I needed him to accept me. Unlike the fabled story, the unrequited childlike beauty I held for a father could not be reciprocated by the beast. The requirements of Harvey's acceptance would plunge me into the dark, twisted, perverted world of a man whose lust-filled, hunger-manifested imagination would send me spiraling down the proverbial rabbit's hole. My childhood would be lost through the looking glass, for I would never see the image of myself the same again.

The experience of an illegal sexual awakening before my time would brand me, scarring and splitting my psyche into a demonic breeding ground ripe for the preparation of my destruction. The springboard from a virtuous childhood into a dangerous cesspool of adulthood would cause the death of my innocence, the theft of my identity, and the destruction of any potential future in my womanhood. I would experience a crack in my reality, causing an inward silence that shattered my spirit, hurling me into a universe that was neither child nor adult. And now, I no longer could relate to either. The unfamiliar, demonic clamor of voices vying for my attention would not allow me peace, only fear. The silence in my world at that time would be deafening.

The resulting anxiety would ferment inside of me. I foolishly held on to it, due to guilt and shame. I would, oftentimes, clearly hear the murmuring sounds of despair reminding me of the failure my adolescence had become. I was sullied. Stuck in the muck of my experience. Held captive by rejection and desire. The rejected desire to be loved by a father. The overwhelming responsibility of secrecy in that silence would trap and betray me. My tormented six-year-old mind could not engage, and others mistook my reticence as timidity. Shortly thereafter, my restraint would be further muzzled by the blast of a gun.

ಒ•ಚ

The following year, my world was turned upside down. After finishing nursing school, Mom was accepted into the United States Air Force as a 1st Lieutenant. She immediately uprooted us from Chicago and drove to Atwater, California, near base, where we would live.

During this time, I realized Harvey quickly faded out of our lives. However, something in Mom had drastically changed. An unspoken abyss subtly crept in between us. The circumstance of her disconnect would also become mine. Most of my memories of her during this time were ones of depression, apathy, and anxiousness. I quietly observed as Mom distanced us from all our family and friends. The thick air of isolation and loneliness was paralyzing.

One sunny California day, I ventured out into my unfamiliar surroundings. I longed to resuscitate what remained of my childhood. Intrigued by the lonesome, slimy trail of a snail next to our townhome's large pool, I decided to follow. I remember wondering, if I removed the snail's protective shell home, would he be as isolated and paralyzed as I was? Or did his slimy trail indicate he had already been secretly wounded, leaving behind evidence of his brokenness? Would the exposure to the unrelenting sun rays leave him scorched beyond recognition? Or would the loss of his calcified barrier leave emptiness? But, something in me took pause. I remembered how defeating it was to be overpowered and ashamed. I recognized the pain that came with being unseen and unnoticed, yet preyed upon. Feeling an obscure connection to my sludgy companion, I instead showed mercy. I do not recall what my seven-year-old mind may have romanticized, as I followed the snail that day, but I could not have imagined how our similar intertwining paths would forever mark the dark, gloomy days ahead.

ಲ•ಆ

I had been banished by my own mother. Mom called my grandmother in Chicago to come to California and pick me up. Grandma dutifully and immediately responded, never questioning Mom's abandonment of Harvey. I imagine Grandma's hope was to reconcile and reestablish their connection. And though she noticed Mom's dissociative and depressive behavior, she did not say as much. Instead, Grandma, grabbing me, did what Mom had asked. Holding tightly to Momma's waist, I sobbed, pleading with her to stay. Dryly, she ordered me back to Chicago with Grandma. I would never see Mother again.

On one of the most heartbreaking days of my life, the inner sanctum of Grandma's apartment would shatter. Although the morning sunshine flooded the room I awoke in, waves of darkness overshadowed me. Despite the heat-soaked blankets on the bed now confining me, I was stone cold. As this strange woman with her strange words spoke to me, I cannot remember when my seven-year-old mind comprehended them. And yet, these same words would be a lasting echo in my young memory.

"Your mother's deceased."

Kinda sounded like she was dead. I raised my small, squinted, barely-woke eyes to gaze at this woman. She looked official. Stoic. Especially now as she sat next to the edge of my bed, pinning me to my fate. The metal pieces on her uniform captured the sunbeams in the windows. The reflection created a prism effect that appeared to bounce off the walls, cascading around the room, as if in angelic announcement. Except the message was not holy, and I was not Jesus' mother Mary. As my eyes searched over her, I recognized the uniform she wore. It was the same one Mom had worn during the ceremony where she was sworn into the United States Air Force as a 1st Lieutenant.

I cannot remember if I asked the woman how Mom had died. I cannot even remember how she told me. Mom had killed herself. Shot herself in the heart. *In. The. Heart.* Those three little words hit with a resounding boom and would resonate within me for a substantial portion of my life. In the flash of a muzzle, in the blink of an eye, she shot out the very organ primarily responsible for pumping the blood needed to oxygenate and sustain her body to live. Literally. Physically. Spiritually.

When I stop to reflect on the moment, I understood Mom was dead. I remember placing my head on this official woman's shoulder, leaning in to let her hug me. Her face gave the appearance of the need for consolation. No doubt a reflection of my own. If she had tried to soothe me, I cannot recall it. I remember feeling an uninvited weightlessness, as if in a nightmare. My lips suddenly quivered overpowered by emotion. Then, shoulders slumped, I wept.

Time ceased to exist. I sat frozen long after the uniformed woman had gone. My grandmother's anguished wailing drifted from the kitchen. I could not soothe her. I was just an insignificant kid with a dead mom. At the time, most of the memories of that day were filed into the survival storage of my unconscious mind. I could not fully recall the file if I wanted to. Searching for it was and is still painful. Death had assured me of it.

I would hear from Harvey only once more. It was not long after Mother's funeral, where I had been rushed to say goodbye, due to the discomfort of onlookers as I kissed her corpse. The phone rang, and I answered. He asked for Isabel, my mother. I remember feeling a coldness rush over me. "She's dead," I said without emotion, and then, with empty satisfaction, slammed the phone back into its cradle. I would never think of Harvey again until the age of twelve.

☽•☾

I remember watching Oprah Winfrey on the carpet of Grandma's living room floor. As Oprah talked of being molested and sexually abused during adolescence, flashes of my corrupted childhood during the time of Mom's relationship with Harvey had broken my memory-filled dam and washed over me like a flood. And so, heavily burdened, I went into the kitchen where some family members were gathered and revealed my secrets in the nonchalant monotone voice of a child intimately acquainted with the rooted effects of death.

The family's shock and horror produced incomprehensible feelings of doubt, fear, confusion, erosion. Eroded security, sanity, and safety, especially when it came to my mother's memory. Grandma's daughter. In the years following, I would endure trips to a child psychiatrist and the unending pitiful looks and stares of the ones who mistakenly thought those same looks and stares would bring any value or insight to the process of my healing. At the time, nothing could help me. The rejection, anger, hatred, bitterness, and rebellion had taken root within the cracked walls of my broken heart. My rage would not be easily satisfied.

I no longer had identity, worth, or value, and I became inconsolable inside. My journey would lead me into the dark, fast-lane world of addiction through a multitude of fleshly desires, including sex, drugs, and alcohol. My rebellion produced in me a violent mistrust and hatred toward those around me. While attempting to find purpose, I became fascinated with the occult world of witchcraft, and I descended into its many layers, exposing myself to volatile situations that would lead to rape, paranoia, and near-death experiences. Slowly, I gave pieces of myself away, embracing destruction, hoping to end the pain of my existence. I knew deep inside my life was worthless, and like Mother, I would never make it past the age of thirty.

On the outside, to others, I appeared to be a young, free-spirited woman having fun, "enjoying" life in all its grandiose experimentation, but my reflection in the mirror spoke otherwise. Inside, I was dark, empty and had no real need for others, who could only provide disappointment and pain. After getting what I thought I wanted, I would walk away, abandoning them the way I had been abandoned.

Years later, I half-heartedly tried to gather the broken pieces of my life by reaching out to my father, whom I barely knew. The next four or so years, through letters and phone calls I could see glimmers of hope at reconciliation and a potential future with my father.

The year 2001, when I was twenty-eight, would prove to be another devastating time in my life, as well as in world history. The year would begin with a traumatic phone call from my half-brother, telling me that our dad was dead. I was in a management class in automotive mechanics at the time, and I remember walking to the middle of the shop, dazed from the news, looking up and thinking, "Not again." I remember the light around me slowly fading into darkness and someone catching me just before I hit the ground, foreshadowing yet another dim future.

༺•༻

After Dad died under suspicious circumstances involving the only son he had raised out of twelve children, the darkness in my life began to consume me from the inside out. I sunk deeper into even darker occultic practices, unbeknownst to those around me, as I delved into the demonic spiritual realm. My first, short-lived marriage would be to a man multi-possessed with the same lustful and perverse demons I had experienced as a child. The mental trauma manifested as physical ailments in my body, producing issues with my reproductive organs and blood. It was as if I were bleeding to death. Literally. Physically. Spiritually.

Six weeks before the New York City 9/11 attacks on the Twin Towers, I dreamed of the event in full color; I wrote it down, telling only a few trusted friends. On the eve of 9/11, I was working on Rush Street in downtown Chicago, where I tended bar. After work, some friends and I decided to drink. That night, I got more drunk than I had in a long time. Before leaving the bar, I distinctly remember seeing four Black males on the street corner, through my drunken starburst halo eyesight, singing a capella. The words of that song would loudly ring out in my ears the following morning.

I awoke on Grandma's couch, not even knowing how I had gotten there from the previous night's alcohol-induced coma. My heavy, bloodshot eyes immediately focused on the television, which was broadcasting live. I could hear Grandma's anxious chatter on the phone in the backdrop. In disbelief, I watched the live news coverage as the first NYC Twin Tower went up in flames with the visible tail of a Boeing 767 billowing smoke. Mouth agape in disbelief, I watched the second plane hit the second tower. The a capella voices from the Boys II Men song cryptically whispered, "It's so hard to say goodbye to yesterday."

The year that would follow can only be explained as an indescribable overflow of unconditional love, support, and encouragement by strategically placed people, miracles, and the almighty hand of God the Father. The spiritually dry and thirsty journey I had traveled my whole life had forced me to its end. Through the faithfulness of one woman, God's true warrior and servant, I was introduced to a church family and experienced a transformative encounter with the Lord Jesus Christ. He saw me like no one else had ever seen me before. He was the father I had always wanted but never knew I needed. He called me by name.

Through the pastors, the study of scripture, counseling, and mentorship by women who not only mothered me, but shared testimony of their own traumatic struggles, I was able to confront my rebellious rage and rejection, unashamed and no longer alone. The demonic torment and sickness I had endured would—through prayers, salvation, and deliverance—eventually transform to inner peace and healing. Under inspiration of the Holy Spirit, I was able to forgive and be forgiven, write poetry and perform spoken word—turning my test into testimony—and minister to others who had gone through similar experiences. Up until this season, I had experienced loneliness, pain, and sorrow and believed that was all I deserved.

But, on January 19, 2003, my thirtieth birthday, which the Lord revealed through Psalm 119, I died. I died a death so pure it would forever transform me by the renewal of my mind, body, and soul, as I witnessed the sacrifice of the One who came to rescue all. The Messiah. The Promised One. He became my rock and strong tower, making me a new creature. A peculiarly wonderful creature capable of seeing past my own shame to love others unconditionally and to fulfill my purpose and destiny as the fire-starter for God's glory.

ABOUT THE AUTHOR

FANNIE OCASIO

Fannie "Firestarter" Ocasio, currently resides in Florida with her husband, children, and grandchildren, working as a detective at the Ocala Police Department. Raised in westside Chicago neighborhoods, she overcame many obstacles through an encounter with the Holy Spirit and professed faith in Jesus Christ. Since 2001, she has served the church, community, and people through youth and women's ministry. She founded Spark a Flame Ministries and Consuming Fire Podcast on Anchor. Visit www.spark-a-flame.org to learn more.

14

RIDE OR DIE

by Wendy Mestas

I was a nineteen-year-old woman, living my life. I had a corporate 9:00-5:00 job working for an insurance broker, making great money with employee benefits and free company trips every summer.

My friend and I decided to go to bartending school and get jobs as bartenders to make money and have something fun to do on weekends during the summer.

My friend said, "I know exactly who will hire us." I met her at a bar with a great view of Downtown Denver. She introduced me to the man behind the bar. "Hey Mark, this is Wendy." He looked up, and as soon as we locked eyes, I felt an instant, powerful, unexplainable feeling that I hadn't felt before.

He hired us and told us to come back next weekend. The bar got really busy, and he was there helping us. He kept touching me on my hips. At the time, it didn't feel inappropriate; it was a light, innocent grip, in which he was showing me he was obviously interested in me.

One weekend, we closed together, and he told his nephew to pour us a shot. I drank with him. One thing led to another, and he carried me to the back to make out.

I told my friend. She was horrified. "You cannot do that! He is married!"

I texted him. "Hey, we cannot see each other, because you are married."

He jokingly responded, "Oh no! We are done!"

I believed him over my friend, so I continued working there. We started hanging out more and more. I was a girl who was just minding her business and who wanted to make money while having fun. I had no idea that I would end up seriously dating him. We would drink and dance like no one was watching. He bought me gifts and made me feel special.

Our relationship moved very fast. Three months after we started dating, he said, "Let's have a baby." I was so young and could not believe he was serious. I didn't think anything of it until, one day, he threw my birth control across the room. I thought, "Is he serious?!" Not wanting to upset him further, I went along with it and ended up pregnant.

One day, when I was about three months along, he was acting very differently. He had been drinking, and I was not happy. We began arguing. I was sitting in the car, and he reached in and wrapped his hands around my neck. I took off. I was completely shocked. I never thought he would try to hurt me, especially when pregnant.

That wasn't the last time, though. He tried choking me again, and I started packing my bag. I told him I was going to go home, and he knelt down and begged me to stay. "Please don't leave me!" I stayed. After all, I was going to have his child.

We ended up getting our own place, and we started our new life together. He was a great cook! He introduced me to new foods, and he taught me how to cook. He was patient, unlike my mother, who would just get upset at my questions. I was his right-hand woman.

Even when we would fight, he had his way of making it up to me. I didn't ask him questions, because he was open about things with me. I believed him. I was trusting. It never occurred to me that he would lie.

When we found out I was pregnant again, we moved from an apartment to a house. One day, after I had my baby girl, he invited his cousin over, and they were drinking. I had to take care of the babies. I heard him upstairs, and he was very belligerent. I could not believe he was acting like that. I did not like his actions and choice of words when he used alcohol.

On Thanksgiving, he started drinking early. I took over finishing dinner and kept with the plans. By the time my mother-in-law came over, he was passed out in the middle of the living room floor. When she saw him, she said, "You should have called me and told me he passed out and canceled dinner!" That option never crossed my mind. I kept it going. I was his ride-or-die.

I started realizing that he had been hiding his drinking problem from me. It didn't stay hidden. He would drink until he passed out on many occasions. I was very upset. We would host every holiday, every kid's birthday party, Superbowl, boxing match, etc. Our place was the party house every weekend. It had turned into a tradition, something that I couldn't stop even if I wanted to. I started realizing that my husband worked Monday through Friday and always partied on the weekend.

At one point, I said to myself, if I can't beat them, I'll join them. But that didn't help. All that frustration from the broken promises built up resentment, and when I would drink, we would fight. He wouldn't back down from me, and it was a really bad combination. I would throw and break stuff in the house. He would punch the wall.

The worst part was my kids would see it. I thought to myself, "This isn't me. Why is he making me feel like this?" I apologized to my step-children, because I got out of character and out of hand. I felt provoked, and I didn't like it at all.

I would sit back and think of our relationship. I realized he had lied to me about his age in the beginning. He had seduced me, fooled me, and blinded me with his gifts. But I stayed with him.

In October 2017, he was diagnosed with rectal cancer. In my mind, I thought, "This is the health scare that will make him stop drinking, and he will turn his life around." We would be one big, happy family. I was hopeful, so I suggested that we get married. We had been together for eight years. "Let's get our mind off the cancer, and let's tie the knot," I said. So, we did. It was the happiest day of my life.

He quit drinking and went through chemo, surgeries, and radiation. On June 5, 2018, he was all done with chemo and radiation. He was cancer free! I thought to myself, now we can start our new and improved chapter.

That dream was short-lived, because he went back to drinking. I was infuriated! I knew that he had no self-control with his drinking. I knew what would happen next. He would change his personality, pass out on the floor, and be hungover the next day. We would spend our Sundays at home, and the binging would start again.

I couldn't believe we had just gone through all that, and now he was going back to the same life. I finally had it; I decided I was not going to live like that. I was scared to leave him, though, because I didn't know where to go. He was the primary breadwinner. We shared the same bank account. I had no savings.

Many nights, I felt lonely and unhappy, because he kept showcasing the same pattern of drinking. I finally got the courage to say, "I am not happy! I am leaving you!" I requested he get me a car to drive my kids to school and practice, and I would figure out the rest. I knew I was okay with my decision and was not afraid anymore, because I was vocal to him about my exit route.

He didn't fight me. He got me a car. Then, right when I was going to leave him, his cancer came back. I thought to myself, there is no way I can leave him. What are people going to say about me? I will be looked upon as a bad wife, mom, and overall woman to leave her husband after his being diagnosed with cancer again. I didn't have it in me to do that, so I stayed.

I stayed, because I wanted to help him. I wanted to make sure he was okay. I was his ride-or-die, once again, even after he disappointed me time and time again. I stayed because I cared, because I loved him. He was the father of my children. I believed it was the right thing to do.

God has a master plan for everything. Right when I was in this crossroad of my life and deciding what and where I was going to go in my new chapter, I was introduced to a financial service company platform, where I could use my professional license in a very special way: teaching families about financial literacy and helping middle American families do what the wealthy do with their money. So, I took the opportunity. Throughout his treatments, I began building my business, taking my laptop to doctor visits, working while being a support system to my husband.

From the day we found out his cancer came back in the liver, we were in and out of the hospital every six weeks, due to continuous infections. This whole experience taught me a lot. Dealing with family, doctors, the unknown, miracles, anger, fear, sadness, and basically every emotion that comes with a terminal illness. I remember my husband saying to me, "You are so gullible! People do not have the same heart as you. There is no white picket fence story!" I knew he couldn't give me the white picket fence life based on the choices he made, but we made it work for our kids. I believe we gave our children the best life we both knew how to provide. Throughout this process, God knew my heart. I did what I was supposed to do as a wife and waited, and I stood by my husband's side—for better or for worse, until death did us part.

Nine months later, my husband passed away. The ugly battle had come to an end. He's in a place where no more suffering or pain exists. We fought together till the very end. I never thought my life with my husband and the father of my children would end like this. We had built a perfectly imperfect life. For a second, I thought a big weight was lifted off my shoulders, but now a new journey had begun: I had to take care of our household and our family without the main provider, protector, and father figure.

This company has brought in a business mentor, coach, and friend, with ten years of experience, who has since been helping me build my business. In the midst of COVID, our CEO stepped up and moved our business online, and I started zooming and booming—all while being a full-time mom, caretaker, and boss building my online business. The best decision I made was to raise my children from the start, which opened doors and brought me to this point in my career.

It was not easy dealing with the fear of COVID, my husband battling cancer, homeschooling, then the passing of the man, who made me a mom and a wife, whom I loved so much and with whom I had built a life that I thought would last until we both grew old and gray. After his passing, all I could think of was what he would say to me: "Get up and don't cry for me. Go out there and continue doing what you've started!" He was so proud of me. Before he passed, he saw me speak, and he told me how proud he was of the wife he had! The journey of this business has allowed me to grow. Once we hit one level, there comes another level to hit and become better than the day before as a leader in business and in our community.

My passion to help families grew even stronger after my loss. Every day, I meet new women from all walks of life, and I get to share my story, which women can relate to, and we build a bond. That is what life is all about, creating relationships with people who understand, appreciate, and respect you and your story.

As an entrepreneur, I shower myself with motivation, affirmations, meditation, and lots of reading for self-development. This has allowed me to lead my team in six different states, because I know I can create my own life. I want to build my empire and not someone else's dream life. The Lord gave me a huge, giving heart, and I know that if I help others get to where they want, I will eventually get what I want and that is to leave a legacy for my descendants. I want them to know who their great-grandmother was and what she gave back to this world to help others.

My goal is to retire my parents by the end of this year, become the youngest Latina broker, teach other women how to become financially free, achieve freedom of time, and become a philanthropist, opening up orphanages and schools and bringing drinking water to places where they need it the most. I want to help provide limitless support and resources for mothers who are struggling financially, emotionally, or physically.

I am on my way to a better version of myself. Some days are tougher than others, but every day, I push myself. Trust me, I have my days where I don't know how I will get through it, but I do it with no shame and allow myself to say, "It's okay to take a mental break for the day." Every day is different, and every day I have my mental battles. However, I want a life free of sickness, and I want my children to have a healthy mom for a very long time.

My husband's passing felt like a big release at first. However, my journey of grieving is still there, and I know it will continue with no expiration date. So, I am aware of how important it is for me and my kids to grieve in the most effective, positive way. I purposely surround ourselves with people that support us in our grief and truly care for our well-being and happiness. And my ultimate goal is to be a better person—better leader, better woman in all areas of life. My financial agency's core values and beliefs focus on the five F's which are faith, family, finance, fitness, and fun. As of now, I believe my life is as good as it gets.

In life and business, I have come to realize that we need to develop thick skin and not to worry about the things we cannot control. Let the haters hate, keep moving forward, show up, share our experiences, and help those who are seeking answers.

My faith is great, and I am learning to lean not on my understanding, but on the Most High God. He is the master to my great plan and the one who knows my true heart's desires. Thinking back now, from day one, there were a lot of red flags. Nonetheless, I was young and naive. Now, I am more aware of what I get myself into. Learning how to say no is still a struggle, because I have a giving heart. But now I make myself available only to the people who reciprocate my energy. I ask a lot of questions, before I jump into something, and think about the possible, long-term consequences. This is key, because we never know what a person can be hiding.

I am thirty-five years young, and I believe God will send me that special someone who has the same goals, ambition, and passion as I do. A man who wants to help me and add value to my life. A man who makes me a priority and wants to see me smile and make me happy and loves my children. I saw a quote the other day, and it's resonating with me as I write this: "Don't be afraid to start over again. This time, you are not starting from scratch; you are starting from experience."

(Some names were changed in the telling of this story.)

ABOUT THE AUTHOR

WENDY MESTAS

Wendy Mestas is a Financial Professional with World Financial Group and an ambitious woman with a goal to become the youngest Latina broker at Pinnacle Agency in Denver, Colorado. The oldest child of Mexican parents who immigrated to America, Wendy is in awe of their hard work. It is her goal to teach those in her community the way money can work. Her agency crusade is "No Family Left Behind." She continues to grow the agency and aspires to leave a legacy for her children. Find her at www.facebook.com/WendyWealth.

15

SEND ME COURAGE IN MY FEAR

by Jeanne Henningsen

Our relationship was perfect on paper. Dan and I had met in college and dated for five years. We liked the same music, enjoyed similar activities. We had even gone to the same church. Yes, there were things I didn't like, but I just thought they were part of his college years. He would mature and change his behavior after we got married, right?

Wrong. Marriage, a great job, even buying a house made no difference. In fact, what I did or didn't like didn't seem to matter. I really wanted a dog. Then, he came home with a feral cat. Maybe a small thing, but a sign of things to come.

He smoked cigarettes, which I didn't like. He also drank, mostly on weekends. Again, college stuff, until the drinking became every night. First, one beer with dinner, then another and another. He would bring an open beer to bed with a back-up on his nightstand, ready to go. If I raised questions, he'd yell, "It's none of your goddamn business! Stop being a nag!"

Next came the drinking after work. Once a week, twice a week, every night. He'd say he'd be home around 7:00 but roll in at 9:00 or 10:00. Soon, it was midnight or later.

There were times we would plan a nice dinner together, complete with candles and dessert. Come 6:00, I would be in the kitchen, ready to serve, and then would wait and wait. Finally, I would eat alone and put the leftovers away. Sometimes, he'd walk in the door before I went to bed, but usually it would be much later. If I said anything, I was again being a nag: "Are you saying I can't go out with my friends? Don't be so difficult." And I would think, he's right. I'm being difficult. So,

I stopped saying anything at all.

I didn't tell anyone what was happening, either. I assumed I was expecting too much. I needed to relax. Then, his moods became more and more unpredictable. I never knew which Dan was going to walk through the door, even when he did come home. Sometimes, he was melancholy and kind of funny. Other times, angry and demanding. Why wasn't the kitchen cleaned? How come his work shirts weren't ironed? That was my job, because I was a woman.

I had to take over paying the bills; late notices and service fees were piling up. The statements showed that he was going out drinking at lunch during work and making regular purchases at a local convenience store after work. Then came bigger charges for electronics, radio-controlled toys, two-handled kites. Our credit card was almost maxed out. I'd tell him we needed to discuss big purchases before making them. That would set him off. How dare I tell him what he can and cannot purchase? He makes the majority of our income. And I thought, he's right. Then, a second credit card came in the mail, and I felt sick.

One night, he came home in a rage, screaming about another thing not being right. He barreled through the kitchen door, kicked away the cat, and before I knew it, the phone was ripped off the wall and was sailing towards me. It hit the wall behind me and broke into a million pieces. I just stood there, trembling. He grabbed his keys and left.

I was left to pick up the pieces, but this time, it felt like something more than just pieces of plastic had broken.

I heard the door open at 2:00 a.m. He didn't come into the bedroom, so I quietly went into the kitchen. He sat there, lights off, pouring himself a whiskey. I flipped on the light, and he jumped. "Leave me alone," he snarled. I began to cry and went back to the bedroom. He followed, apologizing, and he started crying too, saying he knew he was out of control and didn't know what to do. When I suggested he stop drinking and go to AA, he said he just needed to stop during the week.

He tried to stop drinking starting that Monday, but it lasted only one week. By the following week, I was finding empty beer bottles in his car, near his nightstand, and in the trash. Finally, I told him if he didn't come home when he promised, I would be gone. The next week, he didn't come home after work. I packed an overnight bag and headed to a friend's house, where I slept on the couch. It was embarrassing. When I talked with my friend the next morning, the details about Dan's excessive drinking and staying out until early hours of the morning came easily. But I couldn't speak of what hurt more deeply—his words.

When I returned home, I heard lots of these words, yelled at the top of his lungs, "You're so stupid! What did you tell them? Who else did you tell?" I said if he did it again, I would move out. He countered with he was "trying." Again, I offered to go to AA meetings with him, or we could see a therapist. He said he was fine and didn't need any of that.

I wasn't sleeping or eating well. When Dan was home, I felt like I was walking on eggshells. I wasn't sure how much more of his drinking and belittling I could take. The answer to my prayers came in a standard business envelope with a first-class stamp. I was accepted to graduate school.

I had always planned on going to graduate school, because I wanted a career in a different field. I had talked about it with Dan, but he never really listened. When I submitted my application, I had assumed the process would have several rounds, since the program was so competitive. I was stunned when I opened that envelope: an official letter of acceptance to the University of Central Florida Industrial Organizational Psychology graduate program.

With trepidation, I shared the news. Dan immediately lashed out, trying to take control. Why couldn't I just sell candles or jewelry and work from home like some of his colleagues' wives did?

Did I dare send him over the edge with the rest of the news? The campus was in Orlando, and I would have to move there. I wasn't even sure, yet, that I was willing to do that. Again, I prayed. Every night and every morning, I asked for guidance and direction.

My answer came about two weeks later when, once again, he didn't come home. I knew I had to leave for good. This time, I went to my sister's house. I told her everything. She encouraged me to go home to our parents and tell them I had left Dan. I did.

It was so difficult, because I felt like a failure. My parents listened but remained reserved. My father asked if Dan had hit me. When I said no, I could feel his disapproval. I just shut down. Their message was clear: "You have to work hard at marriage." Was I wrong to leave? My gut was telling me no.

That night in my old bed, I slept more than twelve hours with my mother periodically checking on me to make sure I was breathing. When I woke, I ate and ate and ate. I just couldn't get enough. I also wept and told my mother more details. When she saw the whole picture, she immediately said we had to get the rest of my stuff; I was not going back. I knew it was the right decision. It just felt so good to hear her make it for me.

I hadn't recognized the roller coaster I had been riding until I got off. There had been thrilling climbs and good times filled with fun. And I hadn't wanted to fail at one of life's most significant milestones, to lose the fantasy of being happily married, creating a happy home, having children. Yet, when I stepped off that roller coaster, the world stopped spinning. The sick feeling in my stomach vanished.

The next move was to plan my escape. My mother and brother went home with me after Dan had left for work to find he had already changed the locks on what was my house, too! My brother walked around the house and pulled on all the jalousie windows until one popped open. Within moments, he had the door unlocked, and we were in.

The three of us gasped. Just one week after my departure, the house was an absolute mess. The smell was disgusting, a combination of the cat's litter box, dirty dishes in the sink, and an odor I couldn't quite identify. My mother's horrified reaction confirmed it: We had to get me out. We loaded up my brother's truck with the few pieces of furniture that I had brought into our relationship, the rest of my clothes, and some personal items.

I was prepared for his call. He was roaring. How dare I break into his house? I returned, "How dare you change the locks on the house when it's legally mine, too?" With that, he lost it. His words poured out in unbridled fury, a wave of half-articulated insults. I hung up. I was angry, sad, lost.

I accepted UCF's invitation to join the I/O Psychology graduate program. It was official: I was moving to Orlando. I was frightened but also excited. I knew this was the right thing to do.

All alone this time, I returned to the house to retrieve the few items remaining. I dreaded going, knowing he was there. I grabbed my stuff and said goodbye to the cat. I don't remember much else, except Dan's continued attempts—delivered in sobs and shouting—to manipulate and coerce me into believing it was all my fault, that I was giving up. I told him, again, I was willing to go to therapy with him. He said therapy wouldn't fix my problems, because I was psychotic. I headed out the door, his words pelting my back as I walked toward my car. He continued in almost a howl. I kept walking, eyes straight ahead. Once in my car, I looked at him. He just stood in the driveway, watching me leave. Shaking, I drove away, tears streaming down my face.

Three months later, I had moved to Orlando, and Dan had agreed to go into therapy. He even drove the 1.5 hours to Orlando for our sessions, giving me hope that maybe we could work it out. After only six weeks, though, Dan announced that therapy wasn't working. He said, "You haven't changed." He still saw me as the one who needed to be "fixed." He thought if I would just move home, everything would be fine. In my heart, I knew better than that.

Therapy stopped, but phone calls continued. In one call, Dan said I sounded happy. I couldn't deny it. "Yes, I guess I am."

He responded, "If you are happy without me, then you must not love me."

In another call, Dan started with "How can we save our marriage now that you moved away?" This one stung. He was right. I had been the one to move away, to do something for myself. I felt guilty. He sensed an opening and pleaded, "Please come home. I promise things will be different." As much as I wanted to believe him, however, I knew it was another empty promise.

We hung up, and I shuddered with a cry that came from deep within my soul. I felt depleted, broken, and empty. I could not stop sobbing. I lay down on the floor of my apartment and wanted to disappear into it. I wanted the pain to go away. I eventually fell asleep, face down in the piled carpet.

When I woke up, I felt as if I were being lifted up off the floor. I had a renewed strength. I knew someone—God or an angel—was there with me. I stood and looked out the sliding glass doors of my third-floor apartment. From that height, I could see at a distance the pond and its sparkling fountain, and I found myself smiling. No matter how low I felt, I also felt empowered, strong enough to see beyond that moment.

Now, what do I do? There had to be an answer, something better. I retrieved a favorite prayer from my bedroom nightstand. I repeated it over and over. "Help me know that I need not face my troubles alone. Send me consolation in my sorrow, courage in my fear, and healing in the midst of my suffering."

I also thought back to an important conversation I had with my pastor before moving to Orlando. He told me my wedding vows were "for better or for worse," not "for better or for tragic." He also asked me if I would want to have a child who was just like Dan. The clear answer was no. The conversation helped me realize that, even though I had gotten married in the church, it was not a sin to get a divorce. God wanted me to be happy, and that shouldn't be dependent on someone else's decision. Dan made his choice; now I could make mine.

ಬ•ಆ

We got divorced. Dan paid me back my half of the down payment on the house, but soon stopped making the mortgage payments. The house went into foreclosure, and the only thing I got out of it was a bad credit rating. While I recovered, I slept a lot, ate chocolate pudding for dinner, and finally got a dog.

A year after the divorce was final, I graduated with my Master of Science degree and embarked on a new career. I was living on my own, taking care of myself for the first time in my life. My father, though never fully supportive of my decision, said he was proud of me.

I now traveled all over the US and Mexico. This expanded worldview increased my confidence as I navigated through airports, drove a rental car to my destination (without GPS), ate meals by myself, and conducted business meetings on my own. I was discovering who I was and also who I was not. I bought my own brand-new car—a convertible! As the years went by, I started my own business and bought a house.

I had continued therapy for myself for four years. I knew that if I wanted something to be different, I had to be different. Even after therapy, I continued to read self-help books about addiction and codependency. Melody Beattie's books and the workshops at the Kripalu Center for Yoga & Health provided a firm foundation in my healing and personal growth. Even going to the movies by myself, taking myself out to dinner, going to an art show—all these things advanced my self-discovery. When I learned that Dan was arrested twice for domestic violence, I realized that I had forgiven him and had forgiven myself.

Over the years, I had found confidence, strength, and resilience. But what about finding someone to share my life? Could I trust myself to choose someone who would be right for me? Would I recognize manipulation or addiction, when I hadn't recognized it the first time? I dated a lot, thanks to friends, a dating service, and online dating. The variety of dates helped me clarify what I must have in a partner and what would be nice to have. Yes, I had a list. I also had an affirmation that I said every night: "Thank you, God, for bringing this amazing man into my life who loves, cherishes, and respects me for who I am."

And then I met James. I was totally and completely smitten. Talking to him was so easy. Even after thorough searching, I couldn't find any red flags. In fact, I realized he was everything on my list. And I was terrified. Yet, I also recognized that all of my experiences had been shaping me and preparing me to meet James, and my growth would continue with him.

We were thirty-nine years old when we got married. By the following year, I knew I wanted a child. James and I decided that if we did have a child, we would never regret it, but if we decided not to, we might. Six months later, I was pregnant.

At eighteen weeks, we learned we were having a girl. Again, I was terrified. I had screwed up my own life as a young woman. How on earth was I going to raise one? I promised myself that I would be open and honest with Juliana about life, love, and relationships. I would teach her to ask God for guidance and direction, to listen to her intuition, and to be true to herself. I would be there for her when she was heartbroken, made a choice not in her best interests, or felt like she wasn't good enough. No judgment.

I am so mindful that not every woman has access to the resources that I had to help me leave and then grow. This inspired me, in 2016, to start Ignite, a volunteer group of professional leaders who have a passion and deep desire to create a safe and loving community. Ignite works with nonprofit organizations that share our mission, helping them receive funding for and a greater awareness of their cause, including multiple local efforts to aid domestic violence victims, the homeless, and children.

As crazy as it sounds, I am grateful for my early experience. I wouldn't be the person I am today, otherwise. I have learned that difficulties can transform your life, if you only allow yourself to dance in the storm.

ABOUT THE AUTHOR

JEANNE HENNINGSEN

Jeanne Henningsen has been there, done that. She knows all about superwoman capes and the desire to have it all. Jeanne believes women can be focused, grounded, and balanced, which makes them more productive, present, and successful. She has coached hundreds of leaders on releasing overwhelm, finding peace and balance, and discovering their true passions, purpose, and priorities. Jeanne has an M.S. in Industrial Organizational Psychology and is a Certified Professional Coach and a TEDx speaker.

www.ingramcontent.com/pod-product-compliance
Lightning Source LLC
Chambersburg PA
CBHW040243130526
44590CB00050B/4288